COMM0N SENSE BUSINESSMAN AND AUTHOR, JAMES MORROW

HELPED FINANCE EDUCATION WITH FOOTBALL SCHOLARSHIP, LICENSED REAL ESTATE SALESMAN AT AGE 19, GRADUATED IN MARKETING FROM UNIVERSITY OF ALABAMA IN 1964.

REAL ESTATE REPRESENTATIVE FOR SINCLAIR OIL COMPANY PURCHASING SERVICE STATION AND BULK PLANT SITES IN ALABAMA AND MISSISSIPPI IN 1965-1967.

STARTED HIS OWN BUSINESS AT AGE 24. DEVELOPED, SOLD, AND LEASED OVER 100 COMMERCIAL PROPERTIES WHILE OPERATING AND ADVISING PRIMARY BUSINESSES: FURNITURE STORES IN ANNISTON, TUSCALOOSA, MONTGOMERY, MOBILE AND PIEDMONT, ALABAMA.

CREATED JIM MORROW REALTY AND NATIONAL BUSINESS BROKERS.

SOME OF THE NATIONALLY KNOWN BUSINESSES DEVELOPED AND/OR LEASED WERE SEARS ROEBUCK, RED LOBSTER, LOGAN'S ROAD HOUSE, OUTBACK STEAK HOUSE, WINN DIXIE, SINCLAIR OIL COMPANY, WENDY'S HAMBURGERS, HAVERTY'S FURNITURE, RALLY'S HAMBURGERS, AUTO ZONE, COMMERCIAL CREDIT.

ALSO DEVELOPED WERE CHEVRON DISCOUNT MARTS, KFC/TACO BELL, H&R BLOCK, DOLLAR GENERAL, BLOCK BUSTER, WELLS FARGO, SOUTH TRUST BANK, VERIZON, AVIS, MAYTAG, AMERICAN GENERAL INSURANCE, PACIFIC CREDIT, FRED'S, HONEY BAKED HAM, EXPRESS OIL, KRYSTAL'S HAMBURGERS, FAMILY DOLLAR, WAFFLE HOUSE: MCCLENDON FURNITURE, BRIDGES FURNITURE, JEFFERSON HOME, F+M BANK, AND OTHER REGIONAL AND LOCAL BUSINESSES.

AT AGE 58, PURCHASED 471 ACRES IN OXFORD, ALABAMA; CONTRACTED AND NEGOTIATED DEVELOPMENT AND DONATED 180 ACRES TO THE CITY OF OXFORD FOR A GOLF COURSE. LOCATED AND CONTRACTED WITH GOLF COURSE ARCHITECT AND DEVELOPMENT AND MANAGEMENT COMPANY TO CONSTRUCT AN EIGHT MILLION DOLLAR GOLF COURSE AND INITIATE A $11.8 MILLION BOND ISSUE FOR DEVELOPMENT OF THE INFRASTRUCTURE OF 462 LOT RESIDENTIAL DEVELOPMENT, CIDER RIDGE. A TOTAL 20 MILLION DOLLAR PROJECT.

COORDINATED THE CONSTRUCTION OF THE DEVELOPMENT, INCLUDING OVERSEEING SEWER, UNDERGROUND UTILITIES, ROUGH GRADING, BACK FILLING, CURBS AND PAVING. DIRECTED EROSION CONTROL AND ENVIRONMENTAL PROTECTION ISSUES.

MAPPED OUT STREETS AND LOTS WITH THE GOLF COURSE ARCHITECT, SUBDIVIDED THE SIXTEEN NEIGHBORHOODS WITHIN THE DEVELOPMENT, COMPILED PROTECTIVE COVENANTS, LOCATED AND NAMED NEIGHBORHOODS AND STREETS, AND COORDINATED DAILY WITH THE GOLF COURSE CONSTRUCTION, WHILE BUILDING THE SUBDIVISION INFRASTRUCTURE.

SET UP SALES AND BUILDING PROGRAM FOR CIDER RIDGE RESIDENTIAL DEVELOPMENT.

DEVELOPED NO-STRESS FITNESS PROGRAM AND LOST 150 POUNDS IN THE PROCESS. WROTE 3 BOOKS; "LIPSTICK ON A PIG PLUS," "S.O.S. SECRETS OF SUCCESS AND SURVIVAL", "ISOSTRETCH-WEIGHT LOSS, ANTI-AGING FITNESS PLAN." "COMMON SENSE AMERICA NEEDS NOW" IS HIS FOURTH BOOK.".

DEVELOPED AND HOSTED A DAILY RADIO PROGRAM, "COMMON SENSE COMMENTARY."

SEMI-RETIRED, AVAILABLE FOR COMMON SENSE SEMINARS ON SALES, MANAGEMENT, REAL ESTATE, GENERAL BUSINESS, AND WEIGHT LOSS & FITNESS. JIM MORROW

JIM@COMMONSENSECOMMENTARY.COM

THIS BOOK IN SIMPLE <u>COMMON SENSE LANGUAGE</u>, PRINT, AND FORMAT, IS <u>EASY TO ABSORB</u> AND <u>REMEMBER</u>. I THINK IT IS <u>CLOSEST</u> TO <u>FIRST-HAND EXPERIENCE.</u>

WHAT ARE THE <u>WORST PROBLEMS</u> FACING <u>AMERICA</u> <u>TODAY</u>?

IT IS NOT JUST:

"TOO BIG TO FAIL" COMPANIES, MONOPOLIES, TERRORISM, FOREIGN RELATIONS, THE ECONOMY, JOBS, RACISM, LAW AND ORDER, WELFARE, GLOBAL WARMING, ENERGY, POLICE BRUTALITY, DRUGS, EDUCATION, HEALTH AND MEDICAL CARE AND INSURANCE, ABORTION, NUCLEAR PROLIFERATION, GUN CONTROL, SOCIAL SECURITY, NATIONAL DEBT, OR POLITICAL CORRECTNESS.

SOME PEOPLE CALL IT <u>STUPIDITY</u>, AND IT IS SOME.

HOWEVER, IT IS MOSTLY THE <u>LACK</u> OF THE <u>USE</u> OF <u>COMMON SENSE</u> THAT POLITICIANS ARE GUILTY OF, APPROACHING THESE PROBLEMS.

<u>COMMON SENSE</u> MAY GO OUT OF <u>STYLE</u>, LIKE IT HAS IN OUR <u>POLITICS LATELY</u>, BUT <u>IT IS NEVER OUTDATED!</u>

COMMON SENSE IS WHAT MADE AMERICA GREAT, UNIQUE, AND MOST ENVIED IN THE WORLD!

OUR JUDEO-CHRISTIAN BACKGROUND LAWS WERE MOSTLY COMMON SENSE UNTIL THE 1950'S.

SINCE THEN, POLITICIANS HAVE PASSED LAWS AND REGULATIONS THAT HAVE KILLED OUR UNIQUENESS AND DEFIED SANITY!

RELIGIOUS FREEDOM, ALL OF RIGHTS, ESPECIALLY THE RIGHT TO BEAR ARMS, ARE THREATENED BY POLITICAL CORRECTNESS AND LACK OF COMMON SENSE USE!

TWO THINGS CAN BE DONE TO SOLVE AMERICA'S PROBLEMS.

1.AMERICA NEEDS COMMON SENSE NOW!

PEOPLE USED TO LEARN BASIC <u>COMMON SENSE</u> FROM THEIR PARENTS AND <u>YEARS</u> OF <u>HARD WORK.</u>

MOST GOOD PARENTS TODAY, <u>LEARNED GOOD COMMON SENSE</u> FROM WHAT THEIR <u>PARENTS</u> DID <u>RIGHT</u>, OR IN SOME CASES; DID <u>WRONG</u>, WHEN THEY WERE KIDS.

NOW, A LOT OF PEOPLE LEARN "<u>STREET</u> SENSE"; SOME <u>GOOD</u>; SOME <u>BAD</u>: SOME <u>FATAL</u>!

A LOT OF AMERICANS HAVE BEEN RAISED THINKING <u>THAT THEY KNOW EVERYTHING</u>; AND BELIEVING THAT <u>EVERYONE OVER 35</u> IS <u>STUPID</u>!

THESE PEOPLE ARE <u>NOW BECOMING PARENTS THEMSELVES</u>, AND <u>NEED TO LEARN</u>, AND <u>TEACH THEIR KIDS, THAT <u>NO ONE IS EVER TOO YOUNG</u> OR TOO <u>OLD</u> TO USE <u>COMMON SENSE.</u>

YOU <u>DON'T BECOME A GOOD PARENT</u> JUST BECAUSE YOU GET MARRIED AND <u>HAVE KIDS.</u> <u>COMMON SENSE</u> MUST BE <u>USED</u> AND <u>PASSED ON</u> TO

CHILDREN.

 MANY PEOPLE ARE DEPRIVED OF WELL-ROUNDED EXPOSURE TO COMMON SENSE FROM PARENTS, OR YEARS OF "REAL WORLD" WORK EXPERIENCE. I AM TRYING TO PRODUCE THE NEXT-BEST THING IN THIS BOOK!

I AM TRYING TO "EXPOSE" MY 50 YEARS OF COMMON SENSE EXPERIENCE TO AMERICANS WHO HAVE MISSED IT.

NO ONE CAN "MAKE" ANYONE ELSE USE COMMON SENSE.

THEY HAVE TO BE EXPOSED TO IT AND DECIDE WHAT COMMON SENSE IS BEST FOR THEM. (USUALLY BY TRIAL AND ERROR, AFTER BEING "EXPOSED").

EVEN SOME SELF-ABSORBED PEOPLE THAT HAVEN'T BEEN "EXPOSED" TO ANY COMMON SENSE; CAN "DISCOVER" THAT IT IS IN THEIR OWN BEST INTEREST, AS WELL AS OTHERS, TO USE

COMMON SENSE IN MOST EVERYTHING.

FOR PEOPLE THAT HAVEN'T USED IT BEFORE; WHAT WILL THIS "NEWLY-DISCOVERED" COMMON SENSE SHOW THEM ABOUT RESPECT AND OTHER PERSON'S VIEWS?

LIFE IS A TWO-WAY STREET GOING BOTH WAYS. YOU HAVE TO GIVE RESPECT TO GET RESPECT.

I WAS FORTUNATE TO HAVE PARENTS, AN OLDER BROTHER, AND OLDER SISTERS. IT TOOK ME PROBABLY LONGER THAN MOST PEOPLE, BUT I LEARNED A LOT OF COMMON SENSE FROM THEM.

SOME WAS LEARNED DIRECT; SOME BY JUST HANGING AROUND, UNTIL IT RUBBED OFF. I AM PROOF THAT IT IS NEVER TOO LATE TO ABSORB COMMON SENSE!

I DID NOT LEARN IT ALL THE FIRST TIME AROUND. LIKE OTHER KIDS, SOME THINGS HAD TO BE LEARNED THE HARD WAY.

I ALWAYS LIKED TO BE AROUND OLDER PEOPLE. I BELIEVE THAT IT IS BECAUSE, IF YOU WATCH CLOSE ENOUGH, SOMEONE OLDER HAS ALREADY DONE WHATEVER MIGHT BEFALL YOU.

I STILL LEARN FROM OLDER PEOPLE TODAY! IT IS GETTING HARDER, BECAUSE THERE AREN'T THAT MANY OF THEM LEFT THAT ARE OLDER.

IF YOU ARE LIKE MOST OF US, AND DID NOT GET IT ALL, THE FIRST TIME AROUND; THIS IS A GREAT REFRESHER COURSE.

IF YOU HAVE SOMEONE THAT YOU WOULD LIKE TO SAVE A LOT OF PAIN, TIME, AND COST; EXPOSE THEM TO THIS BOOK.

THIS BOOK IS THE COMMON SENSE "GOOGLE" OF THE REAL WORLD. IT IS A LIFETIME OF COMMON SENSE PACKED IN A COUPLE OF HOURS.

YOU WILL LEARN WHAT YOU NEED TO KNOW ABOUT THE REAL COMMON SENSE WORLD; NOT THE FANTASY WORLD, THAT YOU LEARN FROM "GOOGLE"!

2. GET RID OF MONOPOLIES

"TOO BIG TO FAIL" COMPANIES HAVE <u>KILLED</u> THE <u>MIDDLE CLASS</u> IN AMERICA. THEY HAVE MADE THE <u>RICH, RICHER</u> AND THE <u>POOR, POORER</u>.

THEY HAVE <u>CRUSHED COMPETITION</u> AND <u>KILLED</u> THE <u>AMERICAN DREAM</u> OF <u>MIDDLE CLASS</u>, AND MAYBE <u>OWNING</u> INDIVIDUAL BUSINESSES; THEREBY <u>GIVING YOU</u>, YOUR <u>FAMILY</u> AND <u>LOCAL LOYAL EMPLOYEES</u>, A <u>DECENT WAGE</u>.

IF PRESENT <u>ANTI-TRUST LAWS</u> HAD BEEN <u>ENFORCED</u>, WE WOULD <u>NOT</u> BE IN THIS <u>ECONOMIC MESS</u>. THE <u>MONOPOLIES</u> CAN AF-FORD TO <u>HIRE LAWYERS</u> AND <u>BRIBE POLITICIANS</u> TO GET BY THE <u>LAWS</u> AND PUT <u>COMPETING FIRMS</u> OUT OF BUSINESS.

LOOK AT EVERYTHING <u>THAT IS WRONG</u> WITH BUSINESS TODAY: <u>RUDE EMPLOYEES</u>, LONG <u>TELEPHONE WAITS</u>, NO <u>JOBS</u>, NO <u>INSURANCE</u>, <u>SHORT HOURS</u>, <u>BAD PENSIONS</u>, <u>NO SATISFACTION</u> BECAUSE YOU <u>CAN'T COMPLAIN TO THE BOSS</u> ABOUT <u>POOR QUALITY</u>, <u>HIGH PRICES</u> OR <u>ANYTHING</u>.

MOST EVERYTHING <u>WRONG WITH BUSINESS TODAY</u> IS CAUSED BY "TOO BIG TO FAIL" <u>BUSINESSES WITH NO COMMON SENSE</u>, AND <u>NO DIRECT ACCESS</u> TO <u>OWNERS</u> WHERE THE <u>COMMON SENSE PUBLIC</u> CAN <u>SHOW THEM</u> WHERE <u>THEY ARE WRONG</u>!

MY <u>REAL EXPERIENCE</u> WITH NEW YORK "TOO BIG TO FAIL" BANKERS <u>PROVE THE NEED</u>. THEY <u>DECLARED</u> OUR CORPORATION IN <u>DEFAULT</u>; AND <u>SEVERAL</u> OF <u>OUR ATTORNEYS</u> SAID THAT WE COULD <u>PROBABLY WIN THE LAWSUIT</u>.

HOWEVER, THEY SAID THAT IT WOULD TAKE <u>ABOUT 5 YEARS</u> AND A MILLION DOLLARS. <u>WE HAD</u> OVER A MILLION <u>AT THE TIME</u>, THAT THE <u>BANKS CONTROLLED</u>, BUT THEY <u>WOULD NOT LET US HAVE IT.</u>

<u>I FOUND LATER</u> WHY THEY <u>DELIBERATELY</u> CAUSED OUR PROJECT <u>TO FAIL</u>, WHEN WE ONLY <u>NEEDED ABOUT $200,000</u> TO <u>COMPLETE OUR PROJECT</u>, AND WE HAD <u>OVER $1,000,000</u> IN THEIR BANK. THEY HAD DEFAULT INSURANCE PURCHASED WITH OUR OWN MONEY!

<u>THEY GOT</u> THE <u>INSURANCE</u> FOR THE MONEY <u>THEY LOANED US</u>, PLUS AN UP-SCALE <u>NEIGHBORHOOD OF 400 PLUS LOTS</u> SURROUNDING <u>CIDER RIDGE, A PROFESSIONAL GOLF COURSE;</u> <u>FIFTH RANKED IN ALABAMA.</u>

CIDER RIDGE, WORTH <u>MILLIONS AND MILLIONS</u> OF DOLLARS, DEVELOPED BY MYSELF AND <u>FOUR OTHER SMALL</u> LOCAL BUSINESSMEN, <u>WAS TAKEN</u> BY "TOO BIG TO FAIL" MONOPOLIES.

THEY HAVE <u>NO</u> ATTACHMENT, <u>NO LOYALTY</u>, AND <u>NO RESPONSIBILITY</u> TO THE COMMUNITY! IT IS THE SAME STORY ALL OVER THE COUNTRY.

WE MUST <u>RESTORE COMMON SENSE</u> TO AMERICA, AND IMMEDIATELY <u>LIQUIDATE</u> "TOO BIG TO FAIL" <u>MONOPOLIES</u>!

TABLE OF CONTENTS

COMMON SENSE 102--------- SPECIFIC COMMON SENSE SECRETS

ISOSTRETCH IS A "NO SWEAT" FITNESS PLAN OF ISOMETRICS AND STRETCHING.

IT IS RECOMMENDED BY DOCTOR PERRY SAVAGE, FOUNDER OF ALABAMA ORTHOPEDIC SPINE AND SPORTS MEDICINE ASSOCIATES.

THE AMERICAN HEART ASSOCIATION'S STUDY, PUBLISHED IN FEBRUARY 2013, A YEAR AFTER MY ISOSTRETCH DISCOVERY IN MARCH OF 2012, SAID, QUOTE:

"THIS STUDY DEMONSTRATED THAT ISOMETRIC HAND GRIP TRAINING, AND ISOMETRIC LEG TRAINING, RESULTED IN LARGER REDUCTIONS IN SYSTOLIC BLOOD PRESSURE....."

A GREAT TESTAMENT FOR THE "ISOSTRETCH" PLAN! I FOUND THAT MY EXERCISES WERE LOWERING MY BLOOD PRESSURE, A YEAR BEFORE THE HEART ASSOCIATION'S STUDY CAME OUT!

COMMON SENSE HUMOR FROM E-MAILS

COMMON SENSE: "IF YOU'RE GOING TO KILL YOURSELF, DO IT OUTSIDE, I'VE JUST FINISHED CLEANING".

COMMON SENSE RELIGION, "YOU BETTER PRAY THAT COMES OUT OF THE CARPET."

"THE ROAD TO HELL IS PAVED WITH GOOD INTENTIONS!"

COMMON SENSE TIME TRAVEL, "IF YOU DON'T STRAIGHTEN UP,

I'M GOING TO KNOCK YOU INTO NEXT WEEK."

COMMON SENSE <u>LOGIC,</u> "BECAUSE I SAID SO THAT'S WHY".

COMMON SENSE <u>IRONY,</u> "KEEP CRYING AND I'LL GIVE YOU SOMETHING TO CRY ABOUT."

COMMON SENSE <u>STAMINA,</u> "YOU SIT THERE TILL THAT SPINACH IS ALL GONE".

COMMON SENSE <u>ANTICIPATION,</u> "JUST WAIT UNTIL WE GET HOME"

COMMON SENSE <u>HUMOR,</u> "WHEN THAT LAWN MOWER CUTS YOUR TOES OFF, DON'T COME RUNNING TO ME."

COMMON SENSE <u>GENETICS,</u> "YOU ARE JUST LIKE YOUR FATHER."

COMMON SENSE <u>JUSTICE,</u> "ONE DAY YOU WILL HAVE KIDS AND I HOPE THEY TURN OUT JUST LIKE YOU'"

COMMON SENSE <u>WISDOM,</u> "WHEN YOU GET TO MY AGE YOU WILL UNDERSTAND."

COMMON SENSE <u>SIMPLICITY,</u> "I BROUGHT YOU INTO THIS WORLD AND I CAN TAKE YOU OUT."

THIS IS AN EXCELLENT EXAMPLE OF COMMON SENSE, ESPECIALLY IF YOU HAVE NOT BEEN TAUGHT THIS AT HOME.

Live beneath your means. Return everything you borrow. Stop blaming other people. Admit it when you make a mistake. Give clothes not worn to charity. Do something nice and try not to get caught. Listen more; talk less. Every day take a 30-minute walk. Strive for excellence, not perfection. Be on time. Don't make excuses. Don't argue. Get organized. Be kind to people. Be kind to unkind people. Let someone cut ahead of you in line. Take time to be alone. Cultivate good manners. Be humble. Realize and accept that life isn't fair. Know when to keep your mouth shut. Go an entire day without criticizing anyone. Learn from the past. Plan for the future. Live in the present. Don't sweat the small stuff. It's all small stuff.

COMMON SENSE IS KEEPING IT SIMPLE; THE EASIEST AND THE BEST WAY.

DON'T FIX IT, IF IT AIN'T BROKE, AND NOTHING YOU CAN'T SPELL EVER WORKS.

DEDICATED TO MY BROTHER, ALL MY BOYS, MY SISTERS, MY NEPHEWS, MY NIECE, ESPECIALLY MY PARENTS.

BASIC COMMON SENSE 101: COMMON SENSE KIDS AREN'T GETTING TODAY, AND ADULT REFRESHERS: CHAPTERS ONE THROUGH EIGHT.

CHAPTER ONE-101

DON'T ASSUME! FOLLOW UP!

WHY DO NORMALLY SANE PEOPLE, DEVOTED SPOUSES, EVEN COUNTRIES; SUDDENLY BREAK INTO ARGUING, FIGHTING, AND ALL-OUT WAR? THEY ASSUME!

THEY ASSUME THAT WHAT THEY HEARD FROM NEWS REPORTS, RUMORS, OR MOSTLY THEIR OWN EARS, IS TRUE, WITHOUT GETTING THE EXACT FACTS.

IN MY 73 YEARS, EVERY MAJOR PROBLEM HAD TO DO WITH SOMEONE NOT KNOWING THE DANGER OF ASSUMING.

ASSUMING: NOT UNDERSTANDING WHAT WAS SAID; ASSUMING SOMETHING WAS GOING TO HAPPEN AS YOU HAD THOUGHT OR PLANNED.

ASSUMING THAT SOMETHING HAS BEEN DONE IN THE MANNER THAT YOU ASKED; AND NOT FOLLOWING UP TO MAKE SURE OF ITS ACCOMPLISHMENT.

COMMON SENSE SAYS DO NOT ASSUME THAT EVERYONE HEARS AND UNDERSTANDS THE SAME WAY.

EXAMPLE: A BUSINESSMAN, TRYING TO ADD A TOTAL OF A BILL BEFORE HE PAID IT; ASKED HIS PRETTY ASSISTANT:

"YOU WENT TO GEORGIA TECH. IF I GAVE YOU 100,000 DOLLARS, LESS TEN PERCENT, LESS DISCOUNT, HOW MUCH

WOULD YOU TAKE OFF?"

SHE SAID, "EVERYTHING EXCEPT MY EARRINGS!"

THE NEW MURPHY'S LAW: DON'T ASSUME, IF IT IS POSSIBLE TO GO WRONG, IT WILL!

WHAT IS THE "A,#1," MOST COMMON ELEMENT OF FAILURE?

ASSUMING THAT SOMETHING HAS BEEN DONE, WITHOUT FOLLOWING UP, TO MAKE SURE IT HAS BEEN DONE!

IF ANYTHING IS ASSUMED, IT MUST BE FOLLOWED UP TO ASSURE THE JOB HAS BEEN DONE!

IF THE FIRST PRESIDENT BUSH HAD NOT ASSUMED THAT IRAQ'S SADAM HUSSEIN HAD LEARNED HIS LESSON;

IF HE HAD FOLLOWED UP BY FINISHING THE JOB, BILLIONS OF DOLLARS AND THOUSANDS OF LIVES WOULD HAVE SAVED!

IT COULD BE AS SIMPLE AS FOLLOWING UP ON YOUR HAVING TOLD YOUR SON TO TAKE OUT THE TRASH BEFORE THE PREACHER ARRIVES; OR AS CRITICAL AS PRESIDENT BUSH'S MISTAKE.

IF AMERICA DOES NOT FOLLOW UP ON PRESIDENT OBAMA'S ASSUMPTION THAT IRAN WILL NOT MAKE NUCLEAR WEAPONS,

AND NOT ATTACK ISRAEL AND US; THAT WILL BE THE LAST ASSUMPTION ANYONE WILL EVER MAKE!

FOR YEARS, MOST PEOPLE HAVE ASSUMED THAT A COLLEGE EDUCATION WOULD GUARANTEE THEM A GOOD JOB. THEY DON'T ANYMORE!

IF YOU ASSUME YOU WILL MEET AND MARRY THE BOY/GIRL OF YOUR DREAMS BY DOING NOTHING, YOU WILL BE AN OLD MAID OR BACHELOR!

WHY IS ASSUMING ONE OF THE WORST MISTAKES IN SOCIETY?

BY SOMEONE ASSUMING THAT SOMETHING HAD BEEN DONE THAT WASN'T, BECAUSE THEY DID NOT HAVE THE EXACT FACTS!

HOW CAN BATTLES, WARS, FORTUNES, MONEY, MARRIAGES, OR ANYTHING ELSE THAT REQUIRES A SPECIFIC ACTION DONE, BE LOST?

USUALLY, THE ASSUMPTION IS NOT FOLLOWED UP AND MADE SURE THE ACTION WAS DONE. THEN WAR BEGINS!

EXAMPLE: HITLER HAD ASSUMED THAT HIS STAFF WOULD AWAKEN HIM FROM HIS SLEEP IF THERE WAS SOMETHING REAL IMPORTANT GOING TO HAPPEN IN TIME FOR HIM TO REACT TO ANYTHING THAT MAY NEED HIS PERSONAL ATTENTION.

HE WAS WRONG! <u>ON D-DAY</u> (LANDING IN EUROPE WORLD WAR II), <u>HIS STAFF WAS AFRAID TO WAKE HIM</u> UP AND TELL HIM THAT THE <u>ALLIES WERE LANDING IN NORMANDY.</u>

BY THE TIME HE AWOKE, IT WAS TOO LATE TO SEND THE RESERVE FORCES HE WAS HOLDING, TO DEFEND NORMANDY.

IF HE HAD NOT ASSUMED THAT, AMERICANS MIGHT BE SPEAKING <u>GERMAN TODAY!</u>

YOU ALWAYS HEAR ABOUT THE PERSON THAT DROWNED, BY <u>ASSUMING</u> THAT THE <u>WATER</u> OVER THE ROAD WAS NOT DEEP.

YOU SEE MANGLED UP CARS WHERE THEY <u>ASSUMED</u> THAT THEY WOULD <u>MAKE THE CROSSING BEFORE THE TRAIN!</u>

<u>THOUSANDS</u> WOULD BE <u>ALIVE</u> TODAY IF THEY HAD <u>NOT ASSUMED THAT THE GUNS WERE UNLOADED!</u>

MILLIONS <u>ASSUMED</u> THAT <u>STOCK PRICES</u> COULD <u>NEVER FALL</u> AS FAR AS THEY DID AND <u>CAUSE THE GREAT DEPRESSION.</u>

MOST PEOPLE <u>ASSUMED THAT ISLAM</u> WAS JUST <u>ANOTHER HARMLESS</u> RELIGION; UNTIL THEY <u>STARTED BEHEADING PEOPLE!</u>

<u>JFK ASSUMED</u> THAT SINCE A PRESIDENT HAD NOT BEEN <u>ASSASSINATED IN 50 YEARS</u>, THE PARADE IN <u>DALLAS WOULD BE</u>

OK.

EVERYONE ASSUMED THAT THEIR HOUSE WOULD NOT <u>DEPRECIATE</u> SO MUCH <u>AS THEY DID</u> AFTER <u>THE HOUSING CRASH OF 2008.</u>

EVERY DAY IS A NEW DAY WITH A <u>DIFFERENT OUTCOME</u>! JUST BECAUSE IT HAS HAPPENED A CERTAIN WAY IN THE PAST; <u>DO NOT ASSUME IT WILL HAPPEN THAT WAY IN THE FUTURE.</u>

WHAT IS THE <u>REAL REASON</u> WHY PEOPLE <u>MAKE THE SAME MISTAKES OVER AGAIN?</u>

THEY ASSUME THAT IT'S GOING TO WORK RIGHT THIS TIME, <u>WITHOUT FOLLOWING UP</u> TO BE SURE EVERYTHING REQUIRED <u>HAS BEEN DONE.</u>

WHEN BUYING, INVESTING, VOTING, OR EVEN MAKING FRIENDS, <u>DON'T ASSUME</u> WHAT YOU HEAR IS TRUE. <u>ASK QUESTIONS, FOLLOW UP, GET THE FACTS!</u>

THE PEOPLE AND COUNTRIES THAT ARE <u>MOST SUCCESSFUL</u> ARE THE ONES THAT HAVE LEARNED THE <u>COMMON SENSE LESSON</u> OF <u>"DON'T ASSUME, FOLLOW UP!"</u>

HOW CAN YOU KEEP FROM ASSUMING?

DO NOT ASSUME THAT REQUESTED TASKS HAVE BEEN DONE!

ASK!

HAVE THE REQUESTED ACTIONS BEEN DONE?

HOW WERE THEY DONE AND WHEN?

EVEN THEN, IF IT IS IMPORTANT, YOU MUST SEE FOR YOURSELF TO BE SURE.

SEE LATER CHAPTERS ON HOW TO "ASK," & "GET THE FACTS."

CHAPTER TWO-101

WHO YOU KNOW, AND WHAT THEY THINK OF YOU, MAY SOMEDAY BE CRITICALLY IMPORTANT.

IT CAN BE TEACHERS, COACHES, PARENTS, IN-LAWS, STORE CLERKS, AND EVEN FRIENDS. IT CAN BE BUSINESS ASSOCIATES, DOCTORS, EVEN BANKERS.

IT WAS ALWAYS ONE OF THEM I NEEDED MOST IN MY 73 YEARS. LEARN FROM OTHERS' MISTAKES AND SAVE THE PAIN!

EVERY TIME SOMEONE MADE ME MAD, I SAID TO MYSELF, "I WILL NEVER SHOP, USE, ASK, ETC. THEM AGAIN"!

THAT WOULD BE THE VERY PERSON I WOULD NEED

SOME WHERE IN <u>THE FUTURE</u> TO HELP ME!

DON'T <u>MAKE THE</u> <u>MISTAKE</u> OF <u>THINKING</u> YOU WILL <u>NEVER NEED</u> THEM, AND ESPECIALLY; <u>DON'T TELL THEM!</u>

I NEVER THOUGHT ABOUT <u>NEEDING THEM</u>; YOUNG PEOPLE DON'T USUALLY THINK THAT WAY, <u>UNTIL IT IS TOO LATE!</u>

IT TOOK <u>ME YEARS</u> TO <u>LEARN.</u> <u>SAVE</u> THE <u>TIME</u> AND <u>PAIN</u>: <u>USE THE BOOK!</u>

<u>TODAY, 1/8/16</u>, I TOOK AN ITEM TO A <u>CLERK</u> TO <u>ASK THE PRICE</u>. SHE WAS <u>CHEWING GUM</u> SO BADLY THAT I COULD <u>NOT</u> <u>UNDERSTAND</u> <u>WHAT SHE MUMBLED</u>.

I LEFT <u>WITHOUT BUYING</u>; WHEN I WAS <u>YOUNG, I MIGHT HAVE</u> SAID, "<u>I WILL NEVER BE BACK</u>"!

<u>NOW I REALIZE</u> THAT THIS IS THE <u>CLOSEST STORE</u> TO MY HOUSE; I WILL <u>NEED TO BE</u> <u>BACK NEXT WEEK</u>.

DRESSED IN <u>BLUE JEANS</u>, AND <u>OLD HAT</u>; I WENT INTO <u>ANOTHER</u> STORE.

I TRIED TO ASK A CLERK IN THE STORE; "WHERE WAS A CERTAIN EXPENSIVE ITEM"?

THE CLERK WAS PLAYING ON A CELL PHONE; I WAITED FOR MINUTES, THEN FINALLY JUST LEFT!   I WILL BUY THAT EXPENSIVE ITEM SOMEWHERE ELSE!

THAT CLERK DID NOT REALIZE THAT HE WOULD EVER NEED ME UNTIL I TOLD HIS BOSS WHAT HAPPENED.

ANOTHER CASE OF NEEDING SOMEONE IN THE FUTURE:

AFTER BILL OFFENDED HILLARY CLINTON, SHE PROBABLY SAID SOME DOOZIES TO HIM AND HERSELF!

I SAW TODAY 1/8/16, THAT SHE NEEDED BILL TO SAVE HER FAILING CAMPAIGN.

ISN'T IT TERRIBLE THAT SHE HAD TO ASK HIM FOR ANYTHING?

REMEMBER THIS BEFORE YOU SPOUT OFF AT ANYONE, ESPECIALLY PARENTS, SPOUSES, EMPLOYERS, ETC.

WHEN YOU WERE A KID, DID YOU ASK YOUR PARENTS FOR SOMETHING ONE DAY, AND THEY SAID NO?

DID YOU <u>SNAP "FORGET IT"</u>, NOT REALIZING THAT THEY <u>WOULD NOT LET</u> YOU <u>HAVE THE CAR</u> FOR YOUR DATE THAT <u>NIGHT BECAUSE OF YOUR ATTITUDE?</u>

FOR <u>SUCCESS</u> IN YOUR LIFE, YOU WILL NEED <u>MANY PEOPLE, MANY WAYS.</u> USE YOUR <u>COMMON SENSE</u> FOR YOUR <u>OWN SAKE, AS WELL AS BEING POLITE!</u>

CHAPTER THREE-101

<u>MODERATION</u>   <u>MODERATION</u>   <u>MODERATION</u>!

MOST OF LIFE'S SUFFERING IS <u>DUE TO EXCESS</u>-<u>TOO MUCH</u> OR <u>TOO LITTLE</u>.

<u>TIME</u> DOES WONDERS FOR <u>MODERATION</u>. I HAD AS MANY PROBLEMS, WHEN A KID AS MOST TEENAGERS, AND PROBABLY MORE.

PEOPLE, ESPECIALLY TEENAGERS, COME ACROSS PROBLEMS <u>THEY HAVE NEVER SEEN</u>, AND <u>THINK</u> THE PROBLEMS ARE <u>MORE CRITICAL</u> THAN THEY REALLY ARE AT THAT <u>EXACT MOMENT</u>.

WHEN AN EMBARRASSING OR HARMFUL SITUATION HAPPENS, THEY TEND TO MAKE <u>QUICK, DRASTIC</u> DECISIONS THAT MAY <u>HAUNT</u> THEM THE REST OF THEIR LIVES.

MY EXPERIENCE SHOWS THAT MOST OF THESE SITUATIONS <u>HAPPEN AT NIGHT</u>; THERE ARE MANY REASONS WHY.

I HAD MORE THAN ONE OF THESE SITUATIONS, AND WHEN A PARTICULAR SITUATION AROSE, MY WONDERFUL MOTHER TOLD ME <u>NOT TO MAKE ANY IMPORTANT DECISION</u>, ESPECIALLY A LIFE CHANGING ONE, UNTIL I SLEPT ON IT.

TIME HELPS MODERATE EMOTIONS, THUS DECISIONS. I HAVE MADE SOME WRONG DECISIONS, BUT I <u>COULD HAVE MADE MORE SERIOUS</u> ONES, IF I DID NOT HAVE THIS <u>COMMON SENSE ADVICE FROM MY MOTHER</u>.

BECAUSE OF THIS <u>COMMON SENSE</u> THAT SHE PROBABLY <u>LEARNED</u> FROM HER <u>PARENTS</u>, I HAVE MADE MANY MORE CORRECT DECISIONS THAN BAD ONES!

NEVER MAKE AN IMPORTANT DECISION WHEN SOMETHING SEEMINGLY DRASTIC HAS JUST HAPPENED, UNLESS THE SITUATION CALLS FOR IMMEDIATE ACTION.

MY MOTHER SAID, "THINGS ALWAYS LOOK BETTER IN THE MORNING!"

I HAVE SEEN HORSEPLAY OR <u>JOKING CYNICAL COMMENTS</u> TURN INTO <u>FIST FIGHTS</u> AS A <u>KID AND ADULT. DIVORCES EVEN HAPPEN.</u>

THESE MODERATION TIPS COME FROM AN E-MAIL.

THE <u>EFFECTS</u> OF <u>EXCESS ALCOHOL</u> ARE <u>RUINOUS</u> TO THE <u>BODY</u> AND <u>MIND.</u>

<u>TOO MUCH INSTRUCTION</u> LEADS TO <u>LITTLE LEAGUE PARENT SYNDROME.</u>

<u>TOO MUCH LOVE</u> <u>AND FREEDOM</u>, CAN <u>RUIN A PERSON</u> FOR LIFE.

<u>TOO LITTLE DISCIPLINE</u> WILL DO THE <u>SAME</u>.

TOO LITTLE AFFECTION AT HOME HAS SENT <u>SPOUSES</u> <u>ELSEWHERE.</u>

<u>TOO</u> <u>LITTLE LIBERTY</u> LEADS TO <u>REVOLUTION</u>.

<u>TOO LITTLE DESIRE</u> OR DREAMS CAUSE MANY PEOPLE TO <u>NOT</u> <u>REACH THEIR POTENTIAL.</u>

TOO LITTLE PREPARATION LEADS TO **DISASTER**, LIKE THE FELLOW THAT BROUGHT A **KNIFE TO A GUN FIGHT.**

EATING, POLITICS, RELIGION, DRIVING, TASTES, EGO ETC., ARE A FEW OF OTHER THINGS **NEEDED TO MODERATE.**

THIS E-MAIL IS A RELIGIOUS STORY THAT SHOWS COMMON SENSE AND MODERATION. THE **FLOOD STORY** IS IN **MANY RELIGIONS.**

1. **DON'T MISS THE BOAT!**

2. REMEMBER THAT **WE ARE ALL** IN THE **SAME BOAT.**

3. **PLAN AHEAD**; IT WASN'T **RAINING** WHEN THE ARK WAS BUILT.

4. **STAY FIT.** WHEN YOU ARE **600 YEARS OLD**, SOMEONE MIGHT **ASK YOU** TO DO **SOMETHING REALLY BIG.**

5. **DON'T** LISTEN TO **CRITICS**; JUST **GET ON** WITH THE **JOB** THAT NEEDS TO BE DONE.

6. **BUILD** YOUR FUTURE ON **HIGH GROUND.**

7. FOR **SAFETY'S SAKE**, TRAVEL IN **PAIRS.**

8. **SPEED** ISN'T ALWAYS AN **ADVANTAGE**, THE **SNAILS** WERE **ABOARD** WITH THE **CHEETAHS.**

9. **WHEN** YOU'RE **STRESSED**, FLOAT **AWHILE.**

10. REMEMBER THE **ARK** WAS BUILT BY **AMATEURS**; THE **TITANIC** BY **PROFESSIONALS.**

YOU KNOW. IT TOOK ME **55 YEARS** TO LEARN TO SMELL THE

ROSES. EVERYONE NEEDS TO <u>STOP TODAY'S FRANTIC PACE</u> OF DOING THINGS AND <u>SMELL THE ROSES</u>.

 IT'S NOT ONLY <u>GOOD</u> FOR YOUR <u>NOSE</u>, BUT IT'S GOOD FOR YOUR <u>BRAIN</u>.

IF WE COULD GET OUR <u>POLITICIANS</u> TO SLOW DOWN AND SMELL THE ROSES, THEY MIGHT REALIZE THAT THE <u>SIMPLE, COMMON SENSE</u> APPROACH TO <u>ANY PROBLEM</u> IS <u>ALWAYS THE BEST</u>.

AN OLD MAN <u>WAS FUMING</u> BECAUSE HIS SUNDAY PAPER HAD <u>NOT BEEN DELIVERED</u>. HE CALLED THE PAPER, AND AFTER BEING <u>ON HOLD</u> FOR 20 MINUTES, HE <u>BARKED</u> AT THE <u>OPERATOR</u>.

 HE SAID, "WHERE IS THE BLANKETY-BLANK SUNDAY PAPER"? "TODAY IS ONLY SATURDAY SIR". THERE WAS DEAD SILENCE; THEN, "WELL, BLANKETY-BLANK; NO WONDER NO ONE WAS AT CHURCH"!

LISTEN TO THESE COMMON SENSE E-MAIL TIPS.

1. THROW OUT <u>NON-ESSENTIAL NUMBERS</u>, THIS INCLUDES AGE, WEIGHT, AND HEIGHT, <u>LET THE DOCTORS WORRY</u> ABOUT THEM. THAT IS WHY YOU PAY THEM.

2. NUMBER TWO: <u>KEEP ONLY CHEERFUL FRIENDS</u>, THE <u>GROUCHES</u> WILL <u>PULL YOU DOWN</u>.

3. <u>KEEP LEARNING</u>: LEARN MORE ABOUT THE COMPUTER, CRAFTS, GARDENING, WHATEVER. NEVER LET THE BRAIN IDLE, <u>AN IDLE BRAIN IS THE DEVIL'S WORKSHOP</u>.

4. ENJOY THE <u>SIMPLE THINGS</u>.

5. <u>LAUGH</u> OFTEN, LONG, AND LOUD. LAUGH UNTIL YOU <u>GASP FOR</u> BREATH.

6. <u>TEARS HAPPEN</u>. ENDURE, GRIEVE, AND MOVE ON. THE ONLY PERSON WHO <u>IS WITH US</u> OUR ENTIRE LIVES IS <u>OURSELVES</u>. <u>BE ALIVE WHILE YOU ARE ALIVE</u>.

7. <u>SURROUND YOURSELF</u> WITH WHAT YOU <u>LOVE</u>, WHETHER IT'S FAMILY, PETS, KEEPSAKES, HOBBIES WHATEVER. YOUR <u>HOME</u> IS <u>YOUR REFUGE</u>.

8. <u>CHERISH YOUR HEALTH</u>, IF IT IS GOOD, <u>PRESERVE IT</u>, IF IT IS UNSTABLE, <u>IMPROVE IT</u>. IF IT IS BEYOND WHAT YOU CAN IMPROVE, <u>GET HELP</u>.

9. <u>DON'T TAKE GUILT TRIPS</u>. TAKE A TRIP TO THE MALL, EVEN TO THE NEXT COUNTY, TO A FOREIGN COUNTRY, BUT <u>NOT WHERE</u> THE GUILT IS.

10. <u>TELL PEOPLE YOU LOVE</u>, THAT YOU LOVE THEM AT <u>EVERY OPPORTUNITY</u> <u>NOW</u>! ALWAYS REMEMBER; LIFE IS <u>NOT MEASURED</u> BY THE <u>NUMBER OF BREATHS</u> WE TAKE, BUT BY THE <u>MOMENTS THAT TAKE OUR BREATHS AWAY</u>.

ALWAYS USE MODERATION AND LOOK AT THE BRIGHT SIDE:

AN OLD MAN <u>BUMPED</u> INTO <u>ANOTHER OLD MAN</u> AT THE BEACH ONE DAY. HE SAID; "SORRY, I'M <u>LOOKING</u> FOR <u>MY WIFE</u> AND I GUESS I <u>WASN'T</u> <u>PAYING</u> <u>ATTENTION</u> TO WHERE I WAS GOING."

THE SECOND OLD GUY SAYS, "THAT'S OKAY, IT'S A COINCIDENCE, I'M <u>LOOKING</u> FOR <u>MY WIFE TOO</u>. I CAN'T FIND HER AND I'M GETTING A LITTLE DESPERATE"!

THE <u>FIRST OLD GUY</u> SAYS, "WELL, <u>MAYBE I CAN HELP</u> YOU FIND HER. WHAT <u>DOES SHE LOOK LIKE</u>'?

THE SECOND OLD MAN SAID "SHE IS <u>27 YEARS</u> OLD, <u>TALL</u>, WITH <u>RED HAIR</u>, <u>BLUE EYES</u>, <u>LONG LEGS</u>, AND IS WEARING SHORT SHORTS. WHAT DOES <u>YOUR WIFE</u> LOOK LIKE?"

 FIRST MAN SAYS: <u>"DOESN'T MATTER, LET'S FIND YOUR WIFE!"</u>

CHAPTER FOUR (A) 101
K.I.S.S.   KEEP IT SIMPLE STUDENT

MOST PROBLEMS ARE MADE BY PEOPLE NOT UNDERSTANDING EACH OTHER.

THESE PROBLEMS START WITH PEOPLE NOT REALLY INTERPRETING WHAT IS ACTUALLY MEANT BY THE PERSON, OR EVEN NATION, SPEAKING.

BEGINNING WITH PARENT-CHILD, EVEN WITH U.S-RUSSIA, REAL PROBLEMS START WITH A LACK OF EXACT UNDERSTANDING BETWEEN THE PARTIES.

YOU SHOULD MAKE EVERYTHING AS SIMPLE AS POSSIBLE.   K.I.S.S...   KEEP IT SIMPLE STUDENT

EXAMPLE:

FOR A KID TO BORROW THE CAR TONIGHT, HE SHOULD SIMPLY TELL HIS PARENTS:

"I AM GOING ON A DATE WITH SUSAN, AT THE FOX THEATRE, WILL GET A BURGER LATER AT BURGER KING, AND SHOULD BE HOME BY 12 PM."

"IT HAS TO BE TONIGHT BECAUSE "CREED" WITH SYLVESTER STALLONE ENDS TONIGHT AND YOUR CAR IS A LOT NICER".

OTHERWISE, IF YOU JUST SAY "OUT", THEY MAY PICTURE YOU TAKING THEIR NEW CAR DOWN TO THE LOCAL DRAG SPOT, OR WHO KNOWS WHERE, WITH SOME UNSAVORY PEOPLE.

IF SOME EMERGENCY COMES UP, OR YOU ARE LATE COMING IN, THEY WILL NOT KNOW HOW TO GET IN TOUCH WITH YOU.

PUT YOURSELF IN THEIR SHOES. THEY ARE NOT TRYING TO PUNISH YOU.

THEY JUST REALIZE THAT A FATAL ACCIDENTAL DEATH IS FOUR TIMES MORE LIKELY, IN THE 16 TO 22 AGE GROUP, THAN IN OTHER AGE GROUPS.

IF A PRESIDENT WANTS TO INCREASE FOREIGN TRADE AND JUST SAYS HE IS GOING TO VISIT SEVERAL FOREIGN COUNTRIES ON A TRADE MISSION, OTHER COUNTRIES MAY INTERPRET IT, AS THIS:

THEY MAY THINK HE IS GOING TO INCREASE TARIFFS (FEES), LIMIT IMPORTS, TIGHTEN RESTRICTIONS, OR

EVEN DO A LITTLE <u>SPYING AS TO THE COUNTRY'S WAR</u> <u>READINESS.</u>

<u>NO TWO PEOPLE "HEAR" THE SAME THING</u>, THE SAME WAY.   MAKE YOUR STATEMENTS <u>CLEAR, EXACT, SHORT</u> <u>AND SIMPLE.</u>

IN EVERYTHING; PERSONAL, BUSINESS, OR GOVERNMENT; THE <u>SIMPLER, THE BETTER</u>.   THAT IS WHY THIS BOOK IS SHORT.

<u>WHY SHOULD YOU NEVER USE COMPLICATED WORDS OR</u> <u>ACTIONS?</u>

<u>REMEMBER; ANYTHING YOU CAN'T SPELL, NEVER</u> <u>WORKS. K.I.S.S. "KEEP IT SIMPLE STUDENT"</u>!

THE BEST WAY IS THE EASIEST, SIMPLEST WAY!

DON'T FIX IT, IF IT AIN'T BROKE!

WHY IS IT THE GUY DOWN THE STREET SO LUCKY? HE IS <u>NOT AS SMART</u>, NOT <u>AS EDUCATED</u>, NOT AS GOOD LOOKING, <u>AND DOESN'T WORK AS HARD AS YOU.</u>

HE CAN K.I.S.S.- KEEP IT SIMPLE STUDENT!

WHY DO SOME SUCCESSFUL PEOPLE USE THE SAME PRACTICES OVER AND OVER?

THEY BELIEVE IN: <u>"DON'T FIX IT IF IT AIN'T BROKE!"</u>

"REMEMBER-IF YOU'RE SO SMART, HOW COME YOU AIN'T RICH?"

WHY WOULD YOU RE-INVENT THE WHEEL?

NO REASON TO.   LEARN FROM SOMEONE ELSE WHO HAS DONE IT!

WHAT IS THE BEST WAY TO PREDICT THE FUTURE?

BY THE PAST!

WHAT IS THE BEST WAY TO LEARN ANYTHING?

EXAMPLE IS THE BEST TEACHER!

STRIVE TO DO YOUR BEST, BUT DON'T FINE TUNE THE FIDDLE, TILL THE STRING BREAKS!

K.I.S.S.

CHAPTER FOUR (B)101 WRITE IT DOWN.   BE A SELF STARTER.

DEFINITION OF A SELF STARTER IS:

A SELF STARTER IS SOMEONE WHO TAKES THE INITIATIVE.

THEY <u>START</u> TO <u>DO THINGS</u> <u>BEFORE</u> THEY ARE TOLD TO DO SO.

ARE YOU ALWAYS <u>FORGETTING</u> THAT YOU NEEDED TO HAVE DONE SOMETHING? ARE YOU HAVING TO BE REMINDED?

DOES IT FEEL LIKE NOTHING YOU EVER DO, IS RIGHT?

DO YOU FEEL LIKE SOMEONE IS ALWAYS ON YOUR BACK ABOUT SOMETHING?

ARE YOU CONSTANTLY SAYING, "MY BAD!", WHEN YOU REALIZE SOMETHING HASN'T HAPPENED LIKE IT SHOULD HAVE?

DO YOU LOSE INTEREST IN THINGS AND HAVE A "DON'T CARE" ATTITUDE IF EVERYTHING DOESN'T GO RIGHT IMMEDIATELY?

DOES IT SEEM LIKE YOU NEVER HIT A HOME RUN?

GET YOUR FOOT OFF FIRST BASE!

DO YOU THINK YOU ARE ON THE RIGHT TRACK BUT ARE STILL GETTING RUN OVER?

TO NOT GET RUN OVER, STOP SITTING ON THE TRACKS!!

WHAT CAN YOU DO, IF THINGS ARE NOT WORKING OUT, AND YOUR SHIP ISN'T COMING IN?

SWIM OUT TO YOUR SHIP!! SELF START; WRITE IT DOWN!

THE LONGEST JOURNEY BEGINS WITH THE FIRST STEP; WHAT IS THE EASIEST WAY TO LEARN TO TAKE THAT FIRST STEP?

BE A SELF STARTER; WRITE IT DOWN!

IN MAKING DECISIONS: WHAT IS THE WORST THING?

THE BEST THING YOU CAN DO IS THE RIGHT THING;

THE WORST THING YOU CAN DO IS NOTHING.

WHY DO SOME PEOPLE ALWAYS MISS OPPORTUNITIES?
THEY AREN'T PREPARED AND DON'T SELF START.

BE A SELF STARTER; WRITE IT DOWN NOW!

WHY IS KNOWING WHAT TO DO IN ANY SITUATION NOT ENOUGH?

KNOWING WHAT TO DO, WITHOUT ACTION, IS USELESS! BE A SELF STARTER; WRITE IT DOWN!

WHY SHOULD YOU WRITE IT DOWN?

THIS IS NOT TAUGHT IN SCHOOLS, AND MOST PEOPLE NEVER LEARN OF ITS IMPORTANCE.

YOU CAN BE ONE OF THE FORTUNATE ONES IF YOU FINISH THIS BOOK.

WHY WRITE IT DOWN? TO REMEMBER ANYTHING; COMMON

SENSE INCLUDED!

"IF YOU WANT IT TO COME, WRITE IT DOWN; IF YOU DON'T, IT WONT"!

WRITING IT DOWN PUTS A PICTURE IN YOUR MIND; IT BECOMES CLEAR WHEN IT IS WRITTEN DOWN.

YOU ARE A THOUSAND TIMES MORE LIKELY TO REMEMBER WHEN YOU WRITE IT DOWN!

YOUR FRIENDS, RELATIVES, AND BUSINESS ASSOCIATES CANNOT READ YOUR MIND.

"THEY ONLY KNOW WHAT YOUR MOUTH SAYS! YOU ARE WHO THEY THINK YOU ARE"

SOME PEOPLE PICK IT UP BY THE ACCIDENT OF TAKING NOTES IN SCHOOL. OTHERS PICK IT UP THROUGH HARD FOUGHT COMMON SENSE STRUGGLES IN LIFE.

MOST DO NEITHER TODAY; THIS IS THE REASON FOR THIS BOOK.

THE SAD THING IS, THAT MOST PEOPLE DO NOT HAVE AN OPPORTUNITY LIKE THIS. SHARE THIS BOOK WITH AS MANY AS POSSIBLE.

"A PICTURE IS WORTH A THOUSAND WORDS,"

BY WRITING IT DOWN, YOU PUT A PICTURE IN YOUR MIND. YOU ARE A THOUSAND TIMES MORE LIKELY TO REMEMBER!

WHY DO PEOPLE THAT ARE NOT AS SMART AS THE AVERAGE PERSON, HAVE BEAUTIFUL GIRLFRIENDS?

WHY DO THEY HAVE A BIG CAR, AND ARE MORE SUCCESSFUL THAN THE AVERAGE PERSON?

THEY "WRITE IT DOWN" TO REMEMBER THE IMPORTANT THINGS THAT THE AVERAGE GUY DOES NOT!

HOW DO YOU BECOME A SELF STARTER AND WRITE IT DOWN?

BY FORMING A "HABIT" OF WRITING IT DOWN!

USE NEW HABITS THE SAME TIME, SAME WAY, EVERY DAY.

WHEN YOU DO THINGS THIS WAY, <u>THE MOST DIFFICULT</u> THINGS BECOME EASY, BECAUSE <u>YOU ARE USED TO DOING THEM.</u>

THE REASON MOST PEOPLE PUT OFF DOING HARD THINGS IS THAT THEY ARE NOT USED TO DOING THEM AND FIND IT HARD TO START THEM! DO THEM 365 DAYS A YEAR!

MOTIVATION IS EASIER IN THE MORNING AND LESS HARD AS THE DAY GOES ON.

MOST INDISCRETIONS AND CRIMES HAPPEN AT NIGHT! START EARLY!

MAKE A DAILY MEMO OF THINGS THAT MUST BE DONE TODAY! MAKE A REAL EFFORT OF MAKING A HABIT OF DOING THIS DAILY. IT WILL BECOME AUTOMATIC IN A COUPLE OF WEEKS.

WRITE THESE THINGS DOWN OR ENTER THEM ON YOUR ELECTRONIC DEVICE.

WRITE DOWN ALL REQUESTS AND ASSIGNMENTS OF YOUR PARENTS, GRANDPARENTS, SCHOOL TEACHERS, COACHES, AND ANYTHING ELSE THAT YOU THINK IS IMPORTANT,

HOW? SEE BELOW!

USE A 3 BY 5 CARD TO KEEP IN YOUR POCKET OR PURSE TO WRITE THESE THINGS DOWN, OR ENTER THEM ON YOUR ELECTRONIC DEVICE LIKE SO:

1. BRUSH TEETH.

2. FLUSH COMMODE BEFORE LEAVING BATHROOM!

3. CHECK YOUR LIST OF EVERYTHING YOU HAVE TO TAKE TO SCHOOL EVERY DAY.4TAKE PHONE CHARGER WITH YOU.

4. GET TO SCHOOL BEFORE_____.

5. TURN IN REPORT.

6. TAKE NOTES ON EVERYTHING THAT MUST BE DONE FOR CLASS BEFORE TOMORROW.

7. DON'T SKIP LUNCH!

8. DON'T FORGET GLOVES AND MOUTHPIECE FOR SPORTS.

9. ETC., ETC., ETC.

10. DON'T FORGET BACK PACK AT SCHOOL.

11. PUT PHONE ON CHARGE.

12. MAKE A NEW "TO DO" LIST FOR TOMORROW!

HAVE TWO "WRITE IT DOWN" CARDS. ONE "DO IT TODAY" CARD, AND A "GET AROUND TO IT" CARD.

THE "DO IT TODAY" (DIT), CARD IS FOR THINGS THAT ABSOLUTELY HAVE TO BE DONE TODAY, LIKE:

"DENTIST APPOINTMENT TODAY AT 10 AM!

THE "GET AROUND TO IT" (GATI), CARD IS FOR THINGS THAT ARE NOT AS RUSHED, LIKE: "MOM'S BIRTHDAY IS NEXT MONTH." YOU CAN USE YOUR ELECTRONIC DEVICE INSTEAD OF A CARD.

IT IS ESSENTIAL THAT YOU REFER TO THESE, AT LEAST BEFORE THE END OF THE DAY, AND BEFORE YOU GO TO BED, TO MAKE SURE THAT EVERYTHING WAS DONE.

MOVE EVERYTHING TO <u>TOMORROW'S "WRITE IT DOWN" CARD THAT DID NOT GET DONE TODAY.</u>

<u>THEN "MUSCLE MEMORY OF THE MIND" MAKES SELF STARTING AUTOMATIC.</u>

<u>WHAT IS MUSCLE "MEMORY OF THE MIND?"</u>

YOUR MUSCLES REMEMBER TO DO REPETITIVE THINGS WITHOUT REALLY THINKING ABOUT HOW TO DO THEM, LIKE KICKING A FOOTBALL.

YOU DO NOT HAVE TO TELL MUSCLES TO: DROP BALL, RAISE LEG FAST. <u>YOU DO IT AUTOMATICALLY. YOUR BRAIN WORKS THE SAME WAY.</u>

<u>THE MIND IS NO DIFFERENT; DOING IT DAILY MAKES IT AUTOMATIC!</u>

TRAIN YOUR MIND TO BECOME A SELF STARTER, AND DO IMPORTANT DAILY NEEDED ACTIONS EFFORTLESSLY!

<u>ONCE YOUR BRAIN GETS USED TO DOING THIS DAILY, IT BECOMES JUST AS NATURAL AS BRUSHING YOUR TEETH!</u>

I HAVE <u>NEVER MET</u> A CONSISTENTLY <u>SUCCESSFUL</u> MAN THAT <u>HAS NOT</u> <u>LEARNED</u> TO <u>"WRITE IT DOWN!"</u>

CHAPTER FOUR (C) 101 WRITE IT DOWN- SET GOALS TO GET WHAT YOU WANT OUT OF LIFE!

"TO TRAVEL ANYWHERE, YOU MUST FIRST KNOW WHERE YOU ARE GOING! OTHERWISE, YOU WILL WANDER AIMLESSLY ACROSS MANY ROADS."

SET YOUR GOALS FOR WHERE YOU WANT TO GO IN YOUR LIFE, AS YOU WOULD LAY OUT A ROUTE TO SOMEWHERE YOU HAVE NEVER TRAVELED!

YOU MUST RECORD OR "WRITE DOWN" YOUR PROGRESS DAILY AND PUT YOUR FOCUS TOWARD THAT GOAL.

IF YOU CAN IMAGINE IT, YOU CAN DO IT! DIDN'T HENRY FORD HAVE TO IMAGINE THAT HE COULD BUILD A CAR?

IMAGINE IT, MAKE THE COMMITMENT TO WRITE THINGS DOWN NOW, TO BE ABLE TO BECOME A SELF STARTER!

THE DIFFERENCE BETWEEN INVOLVEMENT AND COMMITMENT IS

LIKE <u>HAM AND EGGS</u>; THE <u>HEN</u> IS <u>INVOLVED</u>, BUT THE <u>PIG</u> IS <u>COMMITTED</u>!

UNLIKE THE PIG, <u>ALL YOU HAVE TO DO</u> TO BECOME <u>COMMITTED</u> IS TO BE <u>A SELF STARTER</u> BY <u>"WRITING IT DOWN"</u>!

YOU CAN <u>GET</u> WHATEVER YOU WANT <u>OUT OF LIFE</u> IF YOU BECOME A <u>SELF STARTER</u> BY <u>"WRITING IT DOWN"</u> AND <u>SETTING GOALS!</u>

SEE "BASIC COMMON SENSE 102" FOR GOAL REACHING TIPS!

MOST PEOPLE CAN ONLY REALLY LEARN BY EXPERIENCE; THEREFORE, <u>START OUT WITH SMALL GOALS.</u>

IF IT IS A <u>HARD LESSON,</u> IT WILL NOT BE ENOUGH TO <u>STOP YOU FROM CONTINUING YOUR QUEST!</u>

YOU CAN <u>THEN</u> APPLY IT TO A <u>LARGER SCALE</u> WHEN YOU KNOW <u>HOW TO GET POSITIVE RESULTS.</u>

"SET <u>SHORT</u> GOALS TO <u>BUILD CONFIDENCE, LARGER GOALS</u> FOR LASTING SUCCESS".

SET <u>REALISTIC DEADLINES</u> FOR REACHING THOSE <u>GOALS!</u>

IF YOU DO NOT, <u>YOU WILL NEVER DO IT</u>; YOU WILL ALWAYS

WONDER WHY YOU DIDN'T REACH THOSE GOALS!

EXAMPLE:

SHORT TERM GOAL: MAKE THE FOOTBALL TEAM THAT YOU HAVE ALWAYS WANTED TO PLAY ON BY THE NINTH GRADE.

LONG TERM GOAL: BE THE STARTING QUARTERBACK FOR THAT SAME TEAM BY YOUR JUNIOR YEAR. IT WORKS THE SAME FOR CHEERLEADERS AND MAJORETTES, ETC.

WRITE THESE GOALS DOWN, THINK ABOUT THEM DAILY, AND SET A REASONABLE TIME LIMIT FOR THEM TO BE COMPLETED.

IF NOT, THEY WILL ALWAYS STAY A DREAM OR AN UNOBTAINABLE GOAL.

WRITING IT DOWN ASSURES THAT YOU GET THE EXACT PICTURE OF WHAT IT IS THAT YOU ARE SUPPOSED TO DO, HOW, AND WHEN.

IT ASSURES THAT YOU WILL REMEMBER!

"A PICTURE IS WORTH A THOUSAND WORDS!"

"A PICTURE IS WORTH A THOUSAND WORDS", BECAUSE IT IMMEDIATELY EXPLAINS THE THOUSAND WORDS!

NOTHING BECOMES CLEAR AS A PICTURE UNTIL IT IS DRAWN, OR

"WRITTEN DOWN!"

IT MAKES SURE THAT THINGS THAT HAVE TO BE DONE TODAY, ARE DONE TODAY; OTHERWISE THINGS GET PILED UP, DELAYED, OR FORGOTTEN ALTOGETHER!

IT AUTOMATICALLY MAKES EVERYONE SELF-STARTERS!

IT ALLOWS BETTER TIME MANAGEMENT.

IT BUILDS CONFIDENCE, POSITIVE ATTITUDE, AND YOU ARE READY FOR ANY EVENTUALITY!

YOU CAN GET WHATEVER YOU WANT OUT OF LIFE IF YOU BECOME A SELF STARTER AND BY "WRITING IT DOWN" AND SETTING GOALS!

CHAPTER FOUR (D) 101 WRITE IT DOWN-ALL COMMUNICATION

WHAT <u>CAUSES MOST</u> WORLD WARS, DISASTERS, ARGUMENTS, & FIGHTS <u>AMONG PEOPLE</u>?

<u>LACK OF COMMUNICATION</u>, OR <u>MISUNDERSTANDING</u>, SOMETIMES <u>CAUSED</u> BY HAVING A <u>MIND-SET</u> AGAINST THE OTHER PARTY OR IDEA,

THEN <u>NOT USING COMMON SENSE</u> AND <u>GETTING ALL THE FACTS</u> BEFORE <u>REPLYING</u>!

<u>WHAT IS COMMUNICATION?</u> TALKING, WRITING, EXCHANGING WITH ANOTHER PARTY. THINGS ARE NOT ALWAYS AS THEY SEEM!

<u>YOU MUST LEARN TO READ "BETWEEN THE LINES."</u>

<u>DETERMINE THE EXACT FACTS OF ANY SITUATION BEFORE YOU TAKE ANY ACTION!</u>

SEE CHAPTER ON HOW TO "GET THE FACTS," FOR INSTRUCTIONS.

<u>HOW CAN YOU HAVE BETTER COMMUNICATION WITH PARENTS, TEACHERS, DOCTORS OR ANYONE?</u>

 IT IS IMPORTANT THAT THEY <u>UNDERSTAND</u> EXACTLY WHAT YOUR WORDS ARE SAYING; EVEN <u>THE TENOR</u> OF YOUR VOICE CAN MEAN DIFFERENT THINGS. <u>DON'T RAISE YOUR VOICE!</u>

IF YOU'RE MAD ABOUT ANYTHING ELSE, FAMILY AND FRIENDS WILL THINK YOU ARE MAD AT THEM IF YOU RAISE YOUR VOICE!

SPEAK WITHOUT ACCUSING! ANSWER WITHOUT ARGUING!

WHERE DID THE DAY GO?

HOW CAN I GET EVERYTHING DONE AND STILL BE READY TO DO SOMETHING AT THE END OF THE DAY?

WRITE IT DOWN TO STAY ON SCHEDULE.

ARE YOU HAVING **TROUBLE COMMUNICATING** WITH YOUR **PARENTS, TEACHERS, DOCTORS, ETC.?**

ARE THEY UNDERSTANDING, OR IGNORING YOU?

MOST TIMES, WHEN PEOPLE GO TO DOCTORS, THEY LEAVE WITHOUT TELLING THEM ALL THEY WANTED.

IT CAN BE BECAUSE THE DOCTOR IS RUSHED, **BUT THE SAME THING HAPPENS WITH PARENTS, SPOUSES AND TEACHERS.**

THESE COMMON SENSE SECRETS WILL HELP YOU AND YOUR **DOCTOR DETERMINE EXACTLY WHAT YOUR PROBLEM IS,** AND START YOU ON A QUICK RECOVERY.

WRITE IT DOWN, EXACTLY EVERYTHING THAT AILS YOU: KEEP A LOG FOR DOCTORS, TO HELP THEM DETERMINE THE EXACT PROBLEM AND TO NOT OVERPRESCRIBE.

IF YOU ARE IGNORED, YOU HAVE NOT TOLD THEM, AND THEY DO NOT UNDERSTAND THE EXACT SITUATION.

IF THE COMMUNICATION IS IMPORTANT, WRITE IT DOWN EXACTLY THE WAY YOU WANT TO SAY IT.

THEN HAND THEM THE NOTE, THEY SHOULD GET THE EXACT PICTURE.

YOU DON'T WANT TO GIVE THEM THE IMPRESSION THAT YOU ARE A PEST.

 USE THE NOTE ONLY FOR SELF-MEMORY, UNLESS YOU THINK IT IS IMPORTANT ENOUGH TO GIVE TO THEM!

HOW A PERSON REACTS USUALLY DEPENDS UPON THEIR CIRCUMSTANCES AT THE MOMENT.

THEY COULD HAVE A HEADACHE, HAVE FINANCIAL TROUBLE, BE SICK, ETC.

WITH PARENTS, TEACHERS AND SPOUSES, THERE IS ALWAYS SOMETHING GOING ON TO DISTRACT THEM.

WHAT SHOULD YOU DO, IF YOU THINK SOMEONE IS ACTING UNUSUAL TOWARDS YOU, OR ANY SITUATION?

LOOK AT THE SITUATION AND HOW YOU WOULD REACT. "WALK A MILE IN MY SHOES!"

DO NOT KNEE-JERK TO ANY SITUATION!

NO ONE IS USUALLY COMPLETELY "RIGHT" OR COMPLETELY "WRONG".

IN TALKING OR WRITING, DON'T FORGET YOUR PROMISES!

WHY IS THE WAY YOU COMMUNICATE AND ACT WITH OTHERS, ESPECIALLY YOUR PARENTS, IMPORTANT?

YOU ARE WHO PEOPLE THINK YOU ARE. YOUR **CHARACTER** IS **DETERMINED** BY YOUR **PROMISES!**

WHY SHOULD YOU USE THE COMMON SENSE METHOD OF; **UNDER-PROMISE,** AND **OVER-DELIVER?**

PEOPLE **MAY NOT** REMEMBER THE PROMISES YOU **FULFILLED,** BUT **THEY WILL** REMEMBER THE **PROMISES YOU BROKE.**

THE FIRST PRESIDENT BUSH **WAS DEFEATED** FOR A SECOND TERM BY BILL CLINTON, ONLY **BECAUSE** OF A **PROMISE** HE **MADE** DURING HIS FIRST CAMPAIGN AND **BROKE:** "NO NEW TAXES"!

PROMISE THEM A <u>HAMBURGER</u>, AND GIVE THEM <u>STEAK</u>! THEY WILL REMEMBER IT ALWAYS.

THEY WILL ALSO REMEMBER<u>, IF YOU ARE THE TYPE THAT PROMISES STEAK</u>, AND <u>DELIVERS HAMBURGER!</u>

<u>IT IS BETTER TO UNDER-PROMISE AND OVER-DELIVER!</u>

<u>YOUR CHARACTER</u> (INTEGRITY, HONOR, HONESTY AND MORAL STRENGTH,) IS JUDGED FROM <u>THE WAY YOU FULFILL PROMISES!</u>

<u>THERE IS NO SUCH THING AS A "LITTLE" PROMISE!</u>
YOUR PARENTS ESPECIALLY <u>REMEMBER EMPTY PROMISES.</u>

"I'M SORRY" OR" MY BAD" <u>DOES NOT CUT IT</u> AS A SUBSTITUTE FOR "<u>I WILL DO IT RIGHT NOW</u>, OR "<u>IT WON'T HAPPEN AGAIN!</u>"

IT DOES NOT MATTER IF YOUR PROMISE WAS <u>AS SMALL</u> AS NOT TAKING OUT THE TRASH, OR <u>AS LARGE AS</u>, YOU DID NOT STOP DRINKING AS PROMISED.

<u>NO ONE, ESPECIALLY YOUR PARENTS, WILL TRUST</u>, GIVE YOU MORE RESPONSIBILITY, AND TREAT YOU WITH MORE MATURITY, <u>IF YOU MAKE EMPTY PROMISES.</u>

<u>HOW CAN YOU TO GET WHAT YOU WANT</u> FROM ANYONE?

GIVE THEM RESPECT!

FOR YOU TO HAVE THE RESPECT OF YOUR PARENTS AND OTHERS, YOU MUST SHOW YOUR RESPECT FOR THEM. KEEP YOUR PROMISES!

"THE BUCK STOPS HERE" IS A PHRASE THAT PRESIDENT TRUMAN HAD ON HIS DESK DURING WORLD WAR II.

"PASSING THE BUCK" IS COMMON SENSE FOR SOMEONE PASSING THEIR RESPONSIBILITY FOR FIXING SOME PROBLEM TO SOMEONE ELSE.

TODAY, BECAUSE OF LACK OF COMMON SENSE, A LOT OF YOUNG PEOPLE "PASS THE BUCK," WITH MANY EXCUSES WHY THEY DID NOT GET A CERTAIN JOB DONE.

"NO ONE TRUSTS A "BUCK PASSER."

USE YOUR COMMON SENSE. A BUCK PASSER IN SCHOOL, WILL LIKELY BE A BUCK PASSER IN LIFE.

LIFE IS A NEVER-ENDING TWO-WAY STREET.

TO GET WHAT YOU WANT FROM ANYONE, YOU MUST GIVE THEM WHAT THEY WANT.

THAT INCLUDES YOUR PARENTS, SCHOOL, SPOUSE OR LIFETIME ASSOCIATES.

MUTUAL RESPECT MUST ALSO FLOW TWO WAYS.

PARENTS MUST <u>REQUIRE</u> <u>RESPECTFUL</u> ACTIONS FROM CHILDREN.

ONE OF THE <u>BIGGEST FAMILY PROBLEMS TODAY</u> IS THAT THE <u>CHAIN OF RESPECT IS BROKEN BY EITHER PARENT OR CHILD.</u>

<u>YOU CAN'T TEACH RESPECT</u>, WITHOUT <u>REQUIRING IT FOR YOURSELF</u>; YOU <u>WON'T GET RESPECT</u>, IF YOU <u>DO NOT GIVE IT.</u>

WHEN RESPECT IS <u>GIVEN</u> TO THE CHILDREN AND <u>RETURNED BY RESPECTFUL COMMUNICATIO</u>N TO THE PARENTS; BOTH LEARN <u>MUTUAL</u> RESPECT.

<u>RESPECT, OR LACK OF IT, WILL PASS DOWN GENERATIONS.</u>

CHAPTER FIVE -101 BE PREPARED, OOPS TIME, WORSE CASE SCENARIO

WHAT ARE THE THREE SECRETS THAT CAN HAVE YOU READY FOR ANY EVENTUALITY IN THESE UNCERTAIN TIMES?

BE PREPARED; "OOPS" TIME, AND WORST CASE SCENARIO.

MOST TEEN-AGERS ARE FEARFUL OF SOMETHING HAPPENING THAT WILL EMBARRASS THEM, MAKE THEM LOOK BAD, OR SOMETHING THAT THEY WILL NOT BE ABLE TO HANDLE.

SAVE A LOT OF TROUBLE, COST AND UNHAPPINESS. MAKE THESE THREE EASY PLANS FOR ANY EVENTUALITY.

USE THESE COMMON SENSE SECRETS; BE PREPARED, OOPS TIME, AND WORSE CASE SCENARIO.

LEARNING HOW TO USE THESE SECRETS CAN KEEP A PERSON FROM CONSTANTLY BEING EMBARRASSED, MAKING THE SAME MISTAKE OVER AND OVER, BEING UNABLE TO KEEP FRIENDS AND ACQUAINTANCES, AND NOT BEING ABLE HANDLE CRISES.

WHY SHOULD YOU ALWAYS BE PREPARED?

A SURE-FIRED PRESCRIPTION FOR FAILURE IS NOT BEING PREPARED! YOU CAN LIVE THROUGH ANYTHING IF YOU ARE PREPARED!

WHAT GOES AROUND, COMES AROUND, SO BE PREPARED TO SHIFT GEARS AT ANY TIME.

EVERYTHING IS ALWAYS CHANGING, NOTHING STAYS THE SAME, BE PREPARED!

YOU CAN'T PRACTICE THINGS THAT HAVE TO BE DONE RIGHT THE FIRST TIME!

ALWAYS BE AWARE OF YOUR SURROUNDINGS!

EVERY YEAR, I HEAR ABOUT A KID GETTING HIT WITH A BAT BECAUSE HE ACCIDENTALLY WALKED INTO HIS OWN TEAMMATE SWINGING A BAT!

PEOPLE ARE KILLED TOO OFTEN IN CAR WRECKS BECAUSE THEY DID NOT PAY ATTENTION TO WHAT WAS GOING ON AROUND THEM.

THEY TRY TO ADJUST THE RADIO, TALK ON THE PHONE, OR WERE DISTRACTED BY OTHER PASSENGERS IN THE CAR.

WHAT DO YOU DO IF YOU ARE CAUGHT UNPREPARED?

ALWAYS HAVE A PLAN "B". SEE "WORST CASE SCENARIO" IN LATER PARAGRAPHS.

WHAT IS "OOOPS TIME' AND WHY IS IT IMPORTANT?

"OOOPS TIME" IS ALLOWING TIME TO PREVENT:

"OOOPS, SOMETHING WENT WRONG!"

IT IS IMPORTANT BECAUSE INVARIABLY, <u>SOMETHING UNPLANNED</u> FOR, <u>ALWAYS SEEM TO COME UP</u> AND <u>MAKE YOU LATE</u> OR <u>EVEN MISS SOMETHING IMPORTANT</u> YOU "HAD" TO <u>DO.</u>

AS YOU GET OLDER, THINGS GET MORE IMPORTANT, AND THE PEOPLE THAT YOU DEAL WITH ARE LESS FORGIVING FOR WASTING THEIR TIME.

<u>USE COMMON SENSE SECRET 'OOPS TIME</u>" AT ANY POINT IN YOUR LIFE; BUT, IT'S <u>HARDER</u> IF YOU DO NOT <u>DEVELOP IT IN HIGH SCHOOL & COLLEGE.</u>

IF YOU <u>MUST TURN IN</u> THE PAPER FOR A <u>SEMESTER GRADE</u> BY <u>DECEMBER FIRST</u>, "MURPHY'S LAW" WILL POP UP AT THE LAST MINUTE.

<u>REMEMBER MURPHY'S LAW; "IF IT CAN GO WRONG, IT WILL!"</u>

LEAVE SOME "OOOPS" TIME FOR MURPHY'S LAW!

ALWAYS LEAVE YOURSELF PLENTY OF <u>"OOOPS" TIME</u>. IF THE

WEDDING IS ON SUNDAY, DON'T WAIT TILL SATURDAY TO SEE IF YOUR TUX FITS!

IF THE BIGGEST CONTRACT OF YOUR LIFE IS TO <u>BE SIGNED AT TWO O'CLOCK, BE THERE AT ONE O'CLOCK</u>. NEVER LEAVE TILL TOMORROW</u> WHAT YOU CAN <u>DO TODAY</u>.

<u>WHAT IS THE "WORST CASE SCENARIO" COMMON SENSE SECRET?</u>

LOOK AT ANY PENDING SITUATION. WHEN TRYING TO MAKE A DECISION ON WHETHER TO DO SOMETHING OR NOT; ASK, <u>"WHAT IS THE WORST THING THAT COULD HAPPEN IF I DO THIS?"</u>

IF YOU BELIEVE YOU CAN HANDLE THE WORST THING WITHOUT SIGNIFICANT DAMAGE, <u>YOU WILL BE PREPARED IF IT RESULTS IN A "WORSE CASE SCENARIO"</u>.

IF YOU <u>DO NOT THINK</u> YOU <u>CAN HANDLE THE WORSE</u> THING THAT CAN POSSIBLY HAPPEN IF YOU DO A CERTAIN THING; <u>DO NOT DO IT</u>. SOME THINGS COULD BE FATAL! <u>WHEN IN DOUBT, DON'T!</u>

THE COMMON SENSE SECRET "WORSE CASE SCENARIO" CAN HELP YOU BE A SELF STARTER AND DO THE UNPLEASANT THINGS.

<u>HOWEVER, IF YOU DO NOT CONSIDER THE WORSE CASE SCENARIO, IN MAKING DECISIONS, YOU MAY HAVE A LIFETIME OF REGRET!</u>

CEMETERIES AND PRISONS ARE FULL OF PEOPLE WHO DID NOT LEARN THE COMMON SENSE SECRET OF "WORSE CASE SCENARIO".

IF THE "WORST CASE SCENARIO" DOES HAPPENS, ALWAYS HAVE A PLAN "B".

PLAN IN ADVANCE WHAT TO DO IN THAT CASE.

DO NOT LET IT CATCH YOU LIKE A "DEER IN THE HEADLIGHTS"

IF YOU TURN A SPOTLIGHT ON A DEER AT NIGHT, IT WILL STOP AND FREEZE AND WON'T BE ABLE TO DO ANYTHING.

BY FAILING TO PREPARE, YOU ARE PLANNING TO FAIL!

CHAPTER SIX-101

COMMON SENSE RELATIONSHIPS 101

WHY IS IT IMPORTANT TO USE COMMON SENSE IN YOUR RELATIONSHIPS?

THE WRONG PERSON CAN INFLUENCE ANYONE!!

YOU ARE ONLY AS GOOD OR BAD, AS THE PEOPLE BY WHICH YOU ARE SURROUNDED!

WHAT IS THE COMMON SENSE BASIC OF STARTING AND MAINTAINING A GOOD, HONEST RELATIONSHIP?

MAKE SURE THAT THE OTHER PARTY SHARES YOUR VALUES.

WHAT ARE THE MOST IMPORTANT ATTRIBUTES TO LOOK FOR IN DEVELOPING THESE NEW RELATIONSHIPS?

HONESTY, EMOTIONAL STABILITY, POSITIVE ATTITUDE, AND THE GOLDEN RULE; EMPATHY FOR OTHER PEOPLE!

WHY ARE THESE ATTRIBUTES IMPORTANT?

YOU CAN PUT LIPSTICK ON A PIG, BUT IT IS STILL A PIG!

IF YOU RUN WITH DOGS, YOU ARE GOING TO GET FLEAS.

REMEMBER: "THE PROFIT IS MADE IN THE BUYING, NOT THE SELLING." IF YOU CAN <u>BUY AT THE RIGHT PRICE, YOU CAN ALWAYS SELL ANYTHING.</u>

IN RELATIONSHIPS, <u>IT MEANS</u> THAT IF THEY <u>ARE GOOD, HONEST, MORAL PEOPLE, YOU WILL ALWAYS PROFIT, EVEN IN BAD TIMES!</u>

IF YOU CAN BUY A <u>GOOD COMPUTER FOR $200,</u> IT WILL ALWAYS <u>SELL AT SOMETIME.</u> IF YOU <u>PAID $1000, IT MAY NEVER SELL.</u>

<u>HOW CAN YOU USE COMMON SENSE, TO HELP DETERMINE GOOD RELATIONSHIPS?</u>

COMMON SENSE MUST BE USED IN DETERMINING FRIENDS, SPOUSES, AND LONG TERM EMPLOYEE/EMPLOYER RELATIONS.

<u>YOU MUST HAVE COMMON INTERESTS AND VALUES AT HEART.</u>

BESIDES ALCOHOL AND DRUGS, MOST PEOPLE GET INTO SERIOUS TROUBLE, BECAUSE THEY <u>ARE ASSOCIATING WITH THE WRONG CROWD, (USUALLY OLDER)</u> WHEN SOMETHING ILLEGAL HAPPENS.

ASSOCIATE WITH PEOPLE NEAR YOUR <u>OWN AGE, WITH THE SAME MORAL AND ETHICAL INTERESTS!</u> YOU ARE WHO YOU ARE SEEN WITH!

GOOD GRAMMAR, VALUES AND COMMON SENSE, AND THE FOLLOWING TRAITS, HELP YOU WITH HIGH SCHOOL AND ADULT

RELATIONSHIPS.

THEY COMPRISE THE CHARACTER OF A PERSON.

WHAT IS COMMON SENSE CHARACTER?   PARTS OF COMMON SENSE, MORALS, VALUES, & TRAITS, PICKED UP IN YOUR LIFE.

THE EARLIER THE PARTS ARE PICKED UP, THROUGH LEARNING COMMON SENSE, THE MORE WELL-ROUNDED, YOU WILL BE.

THE MORE OF THESE TRAITS, COMMON SENSE AND VALUES IN A PERSON'S CHARACTER WILL MAKE FOR A BETTER COMPANION.

IF YOU EXPECT THESE FROM SOMEONE ELSE, YOU MUST FIRST OBTAIN THEM FOR YOURSELF.

NO ONE IS PERFECT, BUT HERE ARE SOME OF THE BEST TRAITS, AND COMMON SENSE VALUES:

SELF STARTER, EAGERNESS TO FOLLOW UP

GOOD FACIAL MANNERISMS

FRANK BUT TACTFUL

SENSE OF HUMOR

PLEASANT TELEPHONE VOICE AND MANNERS

COURTESY

TOLERANCE

POSITIVE ATTITUDE

HONESTY

EMOTIONAL STABILITY

FOLLOW INSTRUCTIONS AND NOT ASSUME

ELOCUTION

ATTENTIVENESS

FINISH WHAT IS STARTED

CONFIDENCE

POSITIVE ATTITUDE

INTEGRITY

PERSONALITY

TEMPERAMENT

HONOR

MORAL STRENGTH

APPEARANCE

FLEXIBLE AND VERSATILE

REALIZING THAT "BEING RIGHT" ALL THE TIME IS "WRONG"!

IN ALL RELATIONSHIPS, IT IS IMPERATIVE THAT ALL PARTIES REALIZE THAT BEING RIGHT ALL THE TIME, IS A DISASTER, EVEN IF YOU ARE RIGHT!

DON'T WASTE TIME AND RISK LOSS OF FRIENDSHIP OVER WHO IS RIGHT ON TRIVIAL TOPICS. SAVE YOUR ENERGY FOR TOPICS THAT ARE IMPORTANT!

HOW CAN YOU TELL IF A NEW, YOUNG, ACQUAINTANCE IS GOING TO TURN OUT GOOD OR BAD?

IF THEY DO NOT HAVE AT LEAST <u>HALF OF THE ABOVE QUALITIES</u> AND THE WILL TO <u>OBTAIN THE OTHER HALF,</u> THE CHANCES ARE NOT GOOD.

<u>TO INTEREST PEOPLE</u> IN YOU AND WHAT YOU HAVE TO SAY, YOU MUST ADVERTISE YOURSELF LIKE BUSINESSES ADVERTISE THEIR PRODUCT.

IF YOU DO NOT <u>CAPTURE</u> THE <u>ATTENTION AND INTEREST</u> OF THE <u>DESIRED PERSON</u>, THEY <u>DO NOT</u> REALLY <u>KNOW</u> YOU <u>EXIST</u>.

THERE ARE <u>BASIC RULES FOR ADVERTISING</u> THAT <u>WORK WITH PROSPECTIVE FRIENDS</u> AS WELL <u>AS CONSUMERS.</u>

I USE <u>"H.A.I.R.A.R."</u> TO REMEMBER. H-HOOK, A-ATTENTION, I-INTEREST, R-REASON, A-ACT NOW, R-REPEAT.

YOU MUST HAVE A <u>"HOOK"</u> TO GET THEIR "ATTENTION".

YOU MUST MAINTAIN THEIR <u>"INTEREST"</u>.

YOU MUST GIVE THEM A <u>"REASON"</u> TO BE INTERESTED IN BEING YOUR FRIEND.

THERE MUST BE A REASON FOR <u>"ACTING NOW"</u>.

YOU MUST <u>"REPEAT"</u> THE PROPOSAL TO MAKE IT CLEAR AND REQUIRE ACTION.

EXAMPLE:

<u>"HOOK"</u>—HAVE YOU SEEN THE LATEST CREED MOVIE? USING

MOVIES AS A "HOOK" IS A GREAT WAY TO ATTRACT AND KEEP "ATTENTION" BECAUSE A LARGE PERCENTAGE OF AMERICAN SOCIETY TODAY ENJOY GOING AND WATCHING THE MOVIES.

"INTEREST": IT IS A BOXING MOVIE.

"REASON": IT HAS APOLLO CREEDS SON IN THE MOVIE TRAINED BY ONE OF THE GREATEST TO EVER COME THROUGH THE SPORT.

"ACT NOW": IT IS ONLY SHOWING FOR TWO MORE DAYS.

"ACTION REQUIRED" AND "REPEAT": I AM GOING TO SEE IT TOMORROW. IF YOU WOULD LIKE TO SEE IT, WOULD YOU LIKE TO GO IN THE AFTERNOON OR AT NIGHT?

(NEVER ASK A QUESTION WHERE THEY CAN GIVE A DIRECT "YES" OR "NO".)   THE ANSWER WILL BE 'NO' MOST OF THE TIME!

YOU MUST LEARN THE FOLLOWING BASIC RULES OF GOOD MANNERS AND COMMON SENSE SECRETS FOR THE ABOVE TO WORK!

THE NUT DOES NOT FALL FAR FROM THE TREE. IF YOU WANT TO KNOW HOW YOUR SPOUSES LOOK LIKE IN 30 YEARS, LOOK AT THEIR PARENTS!

TO FIND OUT WHAT TYPE OF PERSON THEY ARE, LOAN THEM MONEY!

DO NOT ASSUME THAT EVERYONE SEES AND KNOWS THE REAL YOU, AND SHARES YOUR VALUES, JUST BECAUSE YOU ARE IN THE SAME CLASS, IN THE SAME CHURCH, OR EVEN WORK WITH THEM.

LOOK AT THEM THROUGH THE EYES OF THE PRECEDING PARAGRAPHS!

BASIC COMMON SENSE 101

CHAPTER SEVEN   GOOD MANNERS, PUBLIC ETIQUETTE, AND OTHER IMPORTANT "HOW TO'S".

MOST OF THE THINGS THAT PEOPLE <u>SHOULD LEARN</u> ABOUT THE <u>COMMON SENSE TRAITS</u> LISTED ABOVE CAN BE LEARNED BY <u>DOING ONE THING</u>.

<u>EVERYONE SHOULD BE REQUIRED TO WORK IN RETAIL OR THE PUBLIC BEFORE GRADUATING FROM HIGH SCHOOL!</u>

<u>THIS IS HARD TO CONVINCE TEENS, BUT, TO HAVE AN ENJOYABLE, HAPPY, SUCCESSFUL FUTURE, THEY MUST LEARN HOW TO DRESS. YOU ARE; WHAT PEOPLE BELIEVE YOU ARE.</u>

<u>IF YOU EVER LOOK LIKE A BUM OR STRIPPER, IT IS HARD TO CHANGE PEOPLE'S OPINION; EVEN IF YOU EVENTUALLY WAKE UP TO THE FACT!</u>

<u>LEARN HOW TO EXPRESS APPRECIATION:</u>

 DON'T LOOK A GIFT HORSE IN THE MOUTH. IT IS THE SENTIMENT THAT MATTERS!

HOW TO MANAGE MONEY:

<u>UNDERSTAND WHAT FINE PRINT IS</u>, AND HOW TO DECIPHER IT, AND HOW CREDIT SCORES <u>CAN AFFECT YOU AND YOUR SPOUSES'</u> <u>FINANCIAL FUTURE.</u>

HOW TO MAKE SMART PURCHASES AND AVOID GETTING SCAMMED?

ASK!

HOW TO USE THE INTERNET PROPERLY (INTERNET MANNERS, ETIQUETTE), ETC.

ASK!

HOW TO DISCERN GOOD INFORMATION FROM BAD?

(MAINLY DETERMINED BY WHERE YOU GOT IT.)

ASK!

HOW TO WRITE A CHECK AND BALANCE A CHECKBOOK?
ASK, WRITE IT DOWN!

HOW TO DRIVE SAFELY.

GOOD DRIVING ETIQUETTE, DWI'S AND SPEEDING TICKETS, COST A LOT OF MONEY AND PHYSICAL AND EMOTIONAL LOSS.

A SPEEDING TICKET IS NEARLY $300 FOR DOING 62 IN A 50 MILE PER HOUR ZONE IN SOME AREAS!

TAKE A SAFE DRIVER'S COURSE AND DON'T BE EMBARRASSED TO USE IT.

DETERMINE IF COLLEGE IS FOR YOU WHILE IN HIGH SCHOOL; DO NOT WASTE TWO OR THREE YEARS IN COLLEGE FINDING OUT.

BASICS OF MOST COMMON RELIGIONS/CULTURES. (ASK, GOOGLE)

HOW TO MAKE A RESUME AND PERFORM WELL AT A JOB INTERVIEW? (COMMON SENSE TIPS IN THIS BOOK.)

HOW TO READ DIRECTIONS AND KNOW WHERE YOU ARE AT ALL TIMES. (GOOGLE)

HOW TO VOTE. (GOOGLE)

BASIC CAR MAINTENANCE. (GOOGLE)

HOW JUMP START CARS, (PARENTS, FRIENDS)

HOW TO MAKE A BUDGET. (PARENTS, CLASS)

THE BASICS OF COOKING, BASIC NUTRITION AND FOOD FACTS. (CLASS, PARENTS, GOOGLE)

FIRST AID/CPR.   (COURSE)

HOW TO DO LAUNDRY   (PARENTS, HOME ECONOMICS)

HOW TO MAINTAIN AN APPROPRIATE LEVEL OF HYGIENE, (PARENTS, DOCTORS, GOOGLE)

GOOD BATHROOM ETIQUETTE.   (PARENTS, GOOGLE)

HOW TO HAVE PRIMARY PHYSICIAN, DENTIST, EYE CARE, AND PREVENTATIVE CHECKUPS   (ASK)

HOW TO BE A SELF STARTER. (SEE SELF STARTING CHAPTER)

WHY AND HOW TO ASK FOR HELP. (SEE ASK CHAPTER)

WHY IS, "IT IS BETTER TO LIGHT ONE CANDLE, THAN TO CURSE THE DARKNESS A THOUSAND TIMES", (OR SOMETHING LIKE THAT!)

THERE IS NO SUCH THING AS A SILLY QUESTION IF YOU DO NOT KNOW THE ANSWER! ASK!!!

DON'T DO SOMETHING, JUST BECAUSE SOMEONE HAS SAID THAT THEY HAVE DONE IT.

IF IT SMELLS BAD, SOMETHING IS USUALLY WRONG WITH IT!

IF YOU THINK THAT SOME ACTION MIGHT HURT YOUR PARENTS OR LOVED ONE, DON'T DO IT! THEY WILL CERTAINLY FIND OUT!

HOW TO MAKE CHANGE AND MAKE SURE THAT YOU COUNT THE CHANGE A BANK OR STORE GIVES YOU.

LEARN WHERE YOUR FOOD REALLY COMES FROM.

LEARN HOW LAND IS TILLED, FERTILIZED, WATERED.

LEARN HOW CROPS HAVE TO USE HERBICIDES TO PRODUCE ENOUGH FOR THE WORLD'S NEEDS.

LEARN HOW WATER, GAS, ELECTRICITY, ETC. IS BROUGHT TO YOUR HOME.

LEARN HOW THE SEWAGE AND WATER ARE TAKEN AND PROCESSED. GOOGLE

LEARN THAT CATTLE MUST BE RAISED AND KILLED FOR STEAKS, ROASTS, ETC. HOGS FOR BACON, RIBS, ETC., AND CHICKENS FOR MEAT AND EGGS.   GOOGLE

LEARN THE REAL COST OF THINGS THAT YOUR PARENTS HAVE TO PAY EVERY DAY FOR YOU!

HOW MUCH IS FOOD, RENT, UTILITIES, GAS, TELEPHONE, CLOTHES CAR, PAYMENTS.   ASK.

LEARN WHERE YOUR PARENTS' MONEY COMES FROM...HOW HARD THEY WORK FOR IT.   ASK

HAVE SOME TYPE OF PAYING JOB, EVEN IF IT IS ONLY CUTTING GRASS, PREFERABLY NOT AT HOME.

LEARN WORK AND ITS REWARDS; AND HOW LONG YOU HAVE TO WORK TO BUY A CERTAIN ITEM.

LEARN HOW TO WORK WITH THE PUBLIC AND OTHER PEOPLE. GET UP AND DO IT!

IF YOU HAVE A CREDIT CARD, MAKE THE PAYMENTS ON IT YOURSELF, EVEN IF YOUR PARENTS HELP YOU WITH MONEY AND "KNOWHOW". YOU NEED TO LEARN THE PROCESS.

MODERATION IN EVERYTHING! DON'T BURN THE CANDLE AT BOTH ENDS! PLAY WITH FIRE, YOU WILL GET BURNED!

KEEP UP WITH HOW OFTEN YOU COMPLAIN. YOU WILL BE SURPRISED.

"ONLY FOOLS COMPLAIN, CONDEMN, AND CRITICIZE, AND MOST FOOLS DO"!

DON'T JOIN IN WITH PEOPLE THAT COMPLAIN ALL THE TIME. YOU WON'T CHANGE THEM. GET AWAY FROM THEM, EVEN IF IT MEANS DIVORCE!

BE POSITIVE! LOOK AT ANY CHORE'S POSITIVE ATTRIBUTES.

DON'T COMPLAIN; DO SOMETHING ABOUT IT!

IF YOU NEED HELP IN LEARNING ANY OF THIS, SEE THE "ASK" CHAPTER IN BASIC COMMON SENSE IO2 SECTION.

YOU MAY BE A REALLY GOOD HONEST PERSON. HOWEVER, PEOPLE WILL JUDGE YOU, AND YOUR FUTURE SUCCESS WILL DEPEND; ON HOW WELL YOU DO MOST OF THE THINGS LISTED IN THIS CHAPTER!

COMMON SENSE 101

CHAPTER EIGHT   NEVER GIVE UP!

WHY SHOULD YOU NEVER GIVE UP WHEN IT SEEMS LIKE NOTHING IS WORKING?

MOST OF THE TIME, IT IS NOT THE SMARTEST, OR THE PRETTIEST THAT SUCCEED: IT IS THE ONE THAT NEVER GIVES UP!

REMEMBER THAT THE MOST OVERALL REASON PEOPLE FAIL AT ANYTHING IS THAT THEY GIVE UP.

HOW CAN YOU AVOID IT, ESPECIALLY IF YOU HAVE FAILED BEFORE?

DON'T CRY OVER SPILLED MILK!

A MAN WHO WON'T QUIT WILL NEVER BE DEFEATED!

COMMON SENSE IS WHY ANYONE CAN GRADUATE FROM COLLEGE. YOU CAN GO AS HIGH AS YOU CAN IMAGINE. ANYONE IS AS GOOD AS ANYONE ELSE AND YOU CAN BE AN "EXPERT".

IF YOU USE COMMON SENSE; NO MATTER HOW BAD TIMES ARE, YOU CAN LEARN TO LIVE THROUGH ANYTHING.

GIVING IN TO BAD TIMES, IS ONLY MIND OVER MATTER.

IF YOU DON'T MIND LOSING, IT DOESN'T MATTER!

HOWEVER, IF YOU DEVELOP A COMMON SENSE POSITIVE ATTITUDE, COMMON SENSE OVERCOMES OBSTACLES.

WHY IS IT BETTER FOR KIDS TO LOSE SOMETIMES?

LOSING IS SOMETIMES THE ONLY THING THAT MAKES HARD LESSONS REMEMBERED!

DON'T SWEAT IT IF YOU ARE NOT THE EARLY BIRD, IT IS THE SECOND MOUSE THAT GETS THE CHEESE!

(THE FIRST MOUSE GETS CAUGHT IN THE TRAP.)

THIS IS THE END OF BASIC COMMON SENSE 101. THIS COMES FROM MY EXPERIENCES, BUT I DON'T CLAIM THAT I LEARNED IT ALL AT AN EARLY AGE.

IN FACT, THERE WERE SOME PEOPLE THAT THOUGHT I WOULD NEVER USE THE COMMON SENSE THAT I LEARNED. I DID NOT DO AS GOOD OF A JOB AS I SHOULD HAVE.

I DON'T EXPECT ANYONE ELSE TO LEARN ALL THIS ON THE FIRST GO-AROUND EITHER, BUT THE EARLIER YOU LEARN AS MUCH AS YOU CAN, THE EASIER AND HAPPIER LIFE YOU WILL HAVE.

SOME OF THE COMMON SENSE SECRETS IN THE FOLLOWING CHAPTERS (102), WERE LEARNED NOT THROUGH SUCCESS AND HAPPY ENDINGS, BUT THROUGH PERSONAL TRAGEDIES AND A MONUMENTAL BUSINESS MISCALCULATION IN MY LATER LIFE.

I HOPE THESE SECRETS WILL GIVE YOU THE SUCCESS I HAD, WITHOUT THE HEARTACHES.

BASIC COMMON SENSE IO2: SPECIFIC COMMON SENSE SECRETS
COMMON SENSE 102

CHAPTER NINE   THE GOLDEN RULE

"DO UNTO OTHERS AS YOU WOULD HAVE THEM DO UNTO YOU."

THIS IS ONE OF THE MOST IMPORTANT COMMON SENSE SECRETS IN PERSONAL, BUSINESS, AND RELIGIOUS RELATIONSHIPS.

MOST PEOPLE THINK OF THIS IN TERMS OF RELIGION. REGARDLESS OF RELIGION, IT IS BASIC COMMON SENSE.

THIS IS THE EASIEST AND SIMPLEST WAY TO ALWAYS BE ASSURED OF DOING THE "RIGHT" THING, NOT JUST IN TERMS OF RELIGION. HONESTY IS ALWAYS THE BEST POLICY!

WHEN SOMEONE SEES THAT YOU ARE GENUINELY INTERESTED IN THEM AND THEIR POINT OF VIEW, THEY ARE MORE COMFORTABLE AND AT EASE WITH THE RELATIONSHIP.

WHAT MUST YOU REMEMBER IN APPLYING THE GOLDEN RULE WHEN MEETING PEOPLE?

IT IS ONLY <u>NATURAL</u> THAT THE <u>NAME</u> ANYONE <u>LIKES TO HEAR MOST</u>, IS <u>OUR OWN</u>. REMEMBER TO <u>USE THEIR NAME</u> AND USE IT <u>OFTEN</u>.

TREATING PEOPLE, <u>THE WAY YOU WANT TO BE TREATED</u> IS THE <u>BASIC COMMON SENSE</u> SECRET <u>TO SUCCESS IN RELATIONSHIPS OR BUSINESS</u>.

WHAT ARE THE <u>THREE MOST IMPORTANT COMMON SENSE SECRETS</u> YOU ABSOLUTELY MUST LEARN FOR SUCCESS?

<u>K.I.S.S.</u>, <u>WRITE IT DOWN</u>, AND <u>THE GOLDEN RULE!</u>

COMMON SENSE 102
CHAPTER TEN   A.B.P.---<u>ALWAYS BE POSITIVE!</u>

<u>THIS IS PRIMARILY COMMON SENSE 101, BUT IS A GOOD REFRESHER FOR ADULTS THAT GET IN A RUT!</u>

<u>ACTING POSITIVE MAKES ONE POSITIVE.</u> YOU HAVE TO START SOMEWHERE. IF YOU "ACT", AND "THINK" POSITIVE YOU WILL BE.

<u>"IF YOU THINK YOU CAN, YOU CAN; IF YOU THINK YOU CAN'T, YOU ARE PROBABLY RIGHT!"</u>

WHAT HAVE <u>PLASTIC SURGEONS</u> LEARNED ABOUT <u>"POSITIVE THINKING?"</u>

PLASTIC SURGEONS HAVE PROVEN THAT PEOPLE WHO REALLY <u>DID NOT HAVE ANYTHING WRONG</u> WITH THEM, IMMEDIATELY BECAME <u>MORE POSITIVE AND CONFIDENT</u> AFTER SURGERY<u>.</u>

WHEN THEY <u>"THOUGHT"</u> THEY LOOKED BETTER, <u>THEY DID!</u>

WHY SHOULD <u>EVERYONE</u> ALWAYS HAVE A <u>POSITIVE OUTLOOK?</u>

<u>NO ONE</u> LIKES A <u>GROUCH</u> OR <u>COMPLAINER!</u>

I LEARNED FROM ZIG ZIGLAR; "ANY FOOL CAN CONDEMN COMPLAIN, AND CRITICIZE, AND MOST FOOLS DO"!

HOW DO YOU ACT POSITIVE AND CONFIDENT IF YOU ARE NOT?

FAKE IT TILL YOU MAKE IT! ACT POSITIVE; CONFIDENCE BREEDS CONFIDENCE!

HOW CAN YOU ACHIEVE YOUR GOALS USING COMMON SENSE POSITIVE THINKING?

COMMON SENSE POSITIVE THINKING MAKES YOU AWARE THAT YOU ARE WHO YOU THINK YOU ARE.

IF YOU THINK YOU CAN, YOU CAN.   IF YOU THINK YOU CAN'T, YOU CAN'T!

COMMON SENSE POSITIVE THINKING SHOWS YOU HOW TO CATCH MORE FLIES WITH HONEY THAN WITH A FLY SWATTER.

 IT MAKES THE WAY TO REACHING YOUR GOALS MUCH EASIER AND FASTER!

WHAT ARE THE BASIC COMMON SENSE SECRETS TO ACCOMPLISHING ALMOST ANY IMPOSSIBLE TASK?

STAY POSITIVE, KEEP TRYING, DON'T GIVE UP!!

COMMON SENSE 102

CHAPTER ELEVEN   EVERYONE IS A SALESPERSON-----

HOW CAN THE FIRST TEN SECONDS DETERMINE YOUR FUTURE AND SURVIVAL?

WHAT IS THE COMMON SENSE PERSONAL TRAIT THAT YOU MUST HAVE, TO BE SUCCESSFUL IN BUSINESS OR PERSONAL RELATIONSHIPS? THE ONE THAT ALMOST NO ONE REALIZES IT'S IMPORTANCE?

EVERYONE IS A SALESPERSON; *A ROCKET SCIENTIST, PLUMBER, A PROFESSOR, AND EVEN PREACHERS.*

ECONOMIC SUCCESS, MARRIAGE, OR EVEN RELIGION, DEPENDS UPON HOW WELL ONE SELLS THEMSELVES.

HOWEVER, EVERYONE IS DIFFERENT; MAKE YOUR DIFFERENCE YOUR OWN!

EVERYONE IS A SALESMAN!

THIS IS 101, 102, AND FOR EVERYONE ON THE PLANET!

WHY HAVEN'T YOU GONE FURTHER UP THE LADDER IN YOUR CHOSEN EDUCATION, BUSINESS OR PROFESSION?

YOU HAVE **NOT SOLD YOURSELF**!

IN SELLING THEMSELVES, **EVERYONE MUST ADOPT** THE *PRINCIPLES OF THE GOLDEN RULE, WALK A MILE IN MY SHOES, AND LEARN THE BASICS OF SALES*. *(BASIC COMMON SENSE)*

IF YOU CAN **TRULY SHOW** THE OTHER PARTY THAT YOU **EXUDE THE GOLDEN RULE** IN **TEN SECONDS**, FINALIZING THE SALE WILL **COME ALMOST AUTOMATICALLY**!

THE "SALE' INCLUDES YOUR RELATIONSHIPS, EVEN YOUR SPOUSE!

WHO ALWAYS GETS **THE BEST JOBS, SPOUSES, AND MOST SUCCESS?**

THE ONES THAT DO THE BEST COMMON SENSE JOB OF **SELLING THEMSELVES.**

ONCE YOU **REALIZE THIS** AND LEARN TO **SELL YOURSELF**, YOU CAN **SELL ANYTHING** AND BE **SUCCESSFUL AT ANYTHING.**

HOW CAN **10 SECONDS** DETERMINE **YOUR FUTURE AND SURVIVAL?**

MOST SALES, INCLUDING **SELLING YOURSELF**, ARE MADE OR LOST **IN THE FIRST 10 SECONDS.** YOU MUST MAKE A **GOOD IMPRESSION IMMEDIATELY.**

THERE IS NEVER A SECOND CHANCE TO MAKE A FIRST IMPRESSION.

HOW CAN YOU KEEP FROM MESSING UP, RIGHT OFF THE BAT?

PUT YOUR BEST FOOT FORWARD IN ANY NEW SITUATION, WHETHER OVER THE PHONE, AT SCHOOL, MEETINGS, ETC.

IF IT IS WORTH DOING, IT IS WORTH DOING RIGHT!

THE FIRST TEN SECONDS WITH THAT ONE PARTICULAR PERSON MAY BE YOUR ENTIRE FUTURE!

WHAT IS THE BIGGEST CAUSE OF PERSONAL AND BUSINESS RELATIONSHIP BREAKUPS?

OVER PROMISING AND UNDER DELIVERING!

THIS WILL UNDERMINE ANY CONFIDENCE THAT ANYONE HAS IN YOU AND YOU MAY NEVER GET IT BACK.

IT IS BETTER TO PROMISE ONLY WHAT YOU KNOW YOU CAN DO; NOT WISHFUL THINKING!

A <u>SMILE</u> IS THE <u>KEY</u> TO <u>OPENING</u> <u>FRIENDSHIPS</u> AND <u>SALES</u>. IT KEEPS <u>FRIENDSHIPS OPEN</u>, AND <u>LOCKS DOWN SALES</u> WITH <u>CUSTOMERS</u> AND <u>RELATIONSHIPS</u>!

COMMON SENSE 102
CHAPTER TWELVE   <u>GET THE COMMON SENSE FACTS</u>

"DO YOU KNOW WHY, THE <u>TOUGHEST GUY IN TOWN</u>; IS LYING ON A SLAB <u>IN THE MORGUE TONIGHT</u>"?

"SOMEHOW, HE DID NOT GET THE FACTS......HE TOOK A LITTLE OL' KNIFE TO A BIG OL' GUNFIGHT.........GET THE FACTS, JACK".

WHAT CAUSES <u>MOST WARS, FIGHTS,</u> AND <u>MISUNDERSTANDINGS</u> IN THE WORLD, AND <u>RIGHT AT HOME?</u>

<u>LACK OF COMMUNICATION,</u> OR <u>MISUNDERSTANDING,</u> SOMETIMES <u>CAUSED</u> BY HAVING A <u>MIND-SET</u> AGAINST THE OTHER PARTY OR IDEA.

THEN <u>NOT USING COMMON SENSE,</u> AND <u>GETTING ALL THE</u> <u>FACTS</u> BEFORE <u>REPLYING</u>!

<u>IF YOU DO NOT HAVE THE EXACT COMMON SENSE FACTS</u> BEFORE YOU COMMUNICATE BY VOICE, PRINT, OR PHONE, <u>A PROBLEM WILL ALWAYS POP UP.</u>

EXAMPLE:

IF YOU PAID THE PHONE BILL AND YOU GET A CALL FROM THE COMPANY SAYING THE BILL IS OVERDUE<u>, DON'T KNEE-JERK</u> AND AUTOMATICALLY ASSUME THAT THEY ARE JUST TRYING TO GET MORE MONEY OUT OF YOU.

<u>THE FACTS COULD BE</u> THAT IT WAS <u>CREDITED TO THE WRONG</u>

ACCOUNT, OR YOU GAVE THE WRONG ACCOUNT NUMBER, OR A MYRIAD OF OTHER THINGS.

BEFORE EITHER PARTY GETS THEIR PANTS IN A WAD, THEY MUST FIND THE EXACT FACTS SO THE MISUNDERSTANDING WILL NOT TURN INTO A REAL PROBLEM.

WARS HAVE BEEN STARTED OVER SIMILAR PROBLEMS THAT SHOULD NOT HAVE BEEN PROBLEMS.

THE EXACT COMMON SENSE FACTS WERE NOT RECEIVED IN THE COMMUNICATION.

DON'T BLOW UP A PROBLEM THAT SHOULD NOT HAVE BEEN A PROBLEM IN THE FIRST PLACE.

AS FOOLISH AS IT SEEMS, A LOT OF FAMILY PROBLEMS START THIS WAY.

IRREPARABLE DAMAGE WILL BE CAUSED IF A NON-PROBLEM EXPLODES INTO A CATASTROPHE!

HOW CAN YOU SOLVE ANY PROBLEM?

FIRST, GET THE COMMON SENSE FACTS AND FIND WHAT IS THE EXACT PROBLEM.

NOT HAVING THE EXACT FACTS, IS LIKE ASSUMING YOU ARE TURNING THE CORRECT WAY ON THE FIRST TURN OF A JOURNEY OF A THOUSAND MILES WITHOUT LOOKING AT A MAP.

YOU COULD HAVE AVOIDED MANY TWISTS AND TURNS, COSTS, AND HEARTACHES, IF YOU HAD THE EXACT FACTS, AND TURNED THE CORRECT WAY.

ONCE YOU HAVE THE FACTS, YOU CAN FIND THE ANSWER TO THE PROBLEM, NEED, OR DEMAND.

USE COMMON SENSE FACTS, NOT WISHES, IN DECIDING ON WHAT YOU PLAN ON DOING NEXT.

WHAT MUST YOU LEARN ABOUT FACTS?

IF YOU DON'T FIND THE EXACT COMMON SENSE FACTS, YOU WON'T BE ABLE TO TELL CHICKEN MESS, FROM CHICKEN SALAD!

GET THE FACTS AND WRITE THEM DOWN TO REMEMBER THEM!

WHY ARE FACTS IMPORTANT?

YOU CAN BE THE SMARTEST, HAVE THE BEST EDUCATION OR

PRODUCT IN THE WORLD, <u>BUT WILL FAIL, IF YOU DON'T GET THE EXACT COMMON SENSE FACTS!</u>

<u>YOU CAN'T GET THERE FROM HERE, IF YOU DO NOT KNOW WHERE "HERE" IS!</u>

<u>THERE IS NO WAY THAT YOU CAN REACH YOUR GOALS WITHOUT THE EXACT FACTS!</u>

<u>HOW CAN YOU GET THE "EXACT, COMMON SENSE " FACTS?</u>

TO GET THE EXACT FACTS, DETERMINE WHAT IS THE ACTUAL TRUTH IN ANY SITUATION. <u>LOOK AT THE OBVIOUS, THEN "LOOK BETWEEN THE LINES."</u>

MANY POLITICIANS SAY SOMETHING LIKE "NO ONE IS GUILTY OF BRIBERY!" <u>(THEN SOFTLY DROP A DISCLAIMER LIKE, "THAT I KNOW OF." OR "IT DEPENDS ON WHAT "IS", IS.)</u>

<u>IN POLITICS, USING OF NOT EXACT FACTS, IS CALLED "SPIN".</u>

<u>YOU HAVE TO ASK SPECIFIC QUESTIONS TO GET FACTS;</u> LIKE, "IF THAT IS THE CASE, <u>WHO EXACTLY EMBEZZLED THE MONEY FROM YOUR CAMPAIGN FUND?"</u>

SOMEONE MAY SAY SOMETHING LIKE, "YOU DON'T BELIEVE I DID LIKE THAT, DO YOU?" HE IS NOT SAYING "YES" OR "NO". HE IS <u>DODGING THE QUESTION, BY "SPINNING!"</u>

THEY DID NOT DENY IT, BUT IT MAY HAVE EVEN MADE YOU FEEL GUILTY FOR ASKING!   <u>READ BETWEEN THE LINES!</u> "EVERYONE SPINS!"

ONE OF THE FIRST STORIES OF NEEDING TO LEARN COMMON SENSE "READING BETWEEN THE LINES<u>," IS IN THE BIBLE, GENESIS 29:27.</u>

LABAN TOLD MOSES THAT HE COULD MARRY HIS DAUGHTER IF HE WORKED FOR LABAN SEVEN YEARS. MOSES DID NOT READ BETWEEN THE LINES.

 MOSES WORKED FOR <u>SEVEN YEARS</u>, AND LABAN TOLD HIM THAT HE COULD MARRY LEAH. HOWEVER, MOSES WAS FOOLED! HE HAD WORKED <u>ALL THOSE YEARS</u> THINKING <u>HE COULD MARRY LEAH'S SISTER, RACHEL.</u>

BECAUSE OF <u>NOT READING BETWEEN THE LINES</u>, MOSES HAD TO <u>WORK SEVEN MORE YEARS</u> TO BE ABLE TO <u>MARRY HIS TRUE LOVE, RACHEL.</u>

<u>TODAY'S GENERATION DOES NOT HAVE THE COMMON SENSE OF THEIR PARENTS.</u>

<u>SCHOOLS ARE PROHIBITED FROM TEACHING STORIES LIKE THIS.</u>

<u>MORAL DECAY AND BREAKUP OF FAMILY LIFE ARE REVOLVING CYCLES THAT CAUSE GENERATIONS TO NOT LEARN COMMON SENSE.</u>

AMERICA WAS FOUNDED ON THESE JUDEO-CHRISTIAN LAWS AND MORALS.   THIS IS NOT A RELIGIOUS SPIN.   IT IS JUST A FACT.

LACK OF THE USE OF COMMON SENSE, MORAL DECAY, AND FAMILY BREAKUP, CAN SPELL THE END OF A NATION, AS WELL AS FAMILIES.

USE COMMON SENSE FACTS TO READ BETWEEN THE LINES IN COMMUNICATIONS, AND IN EVERY DAY EVENTS, ESPECIALLY POLITICS!

CHAPTER THIRTEEN

ASK!

THIS IS SO SIMPLE YOU WOULD THINK THAT IT SHOULD BE 101….

BUT KEEPING IT SIMPLE, OFTEN INVOLVES ASKING! <u>SO IT IS 101 AND 102.</u>

<u>HOW ARE YOU GOING TO FIND OUT THE COMMON SENSE FACTS THAT YOU NEED?</u>

FIRST, OBSERVE WHAT "COMMON SENSE" METHODS ARE USED BY FRIENDS, FAMILY, OR PEOPLE YOU ADMIRE.

<u>OBSERVING IS FINE, BUT MOST OFTEN YOU STILL JUST HAVE TO ASK!</u>

<u>NO ONE IS GOING TO GIVE YOU ANYTHING, IF THEY DO NOT KNOW WHAT YOU WANT!</u>

NO ONE IS GOING TO ASK QUESTIONS FOR YOU!

ASK IN PERSON, OR LOOK IN BOOKS, COMPUTER, ETC.

WHY IS IT BETTER TO ASK, RATHER THAN RISK EMBARRASSMENT BY NOT ASKING?

THERE ARE NO DUMB QUESTIONS; ONLY DUMB PEOPLE FOR NOT ASKING!

IT IS BETTER TO LIGHT ONE CANDLE THAN TO CURSE THE DARKNESS A THOUSAND TIMES!

ASKING IS THE KEY TO GETTING WHAT YOU WANT, WHETHER YOU ARE SELLING A CAR OR SELLING YOURSELF TO A GIRLFRIEND OR EMPLOYER.

IF YOU DON'T ASK FOR IT YOU WON'T GET IT.

IF YOU ARE LOOKING FOR A POSITIVE RESPONSE, ASK A QUESTION THAT CANNOT BE ANSWERED WITH A "NO".

"SHALL I DELIVER IT TODAY OR WILL TOMORROW BE MORE CONVENIENT? WHAT TIME SHALL I PICK YOU UP"

THE SQUEAKY WHEEL GETS THE GREASE!

LISTEN

WHAT IS THE <u>LEAST USED COMMON SENSE</u> THAT MOST PEOPLE KNOW, BUT <u>DO NOT USE WELL?</u>

<u>LISTEN!</u>

DO YOU THINK <u>PEARL HARBOR OR 9/11</u> WOULD HAVE HAPPENED IF SOMEONE IN OUR <u>GOVERNMENT HAD USED THEIR COMMON SENSE AND LISTENED?</u>

<u>WOULD IT HAVE HAPPENED</u> IF SOMEONE HAD LISTENED, <u>READ BETWEEN THE LINES,</u> AND EXPLAINED CLEARLY TO <u>PERSONS RESPONSIBLE FOR OUR DEFENSE?</u>

"IF YOU DO NOT <u>HEED HISTORY</u>, YOU <u>ARE DESTINED TO REPEAT IT</u>"!

WHY SHOULD YOU LISTEN AND "READ BETWEEN LINES"?

LISTENING AND READING BETWEEN THE LINES, WITH COMMON SENSE, IS EVEN MORE IMPORTANT IN YOUR PERSONAL LIFE.

IF YOU HAVE NOT LISTENED CLOSE ENOUGH IN THE PAST, SOMETHING WILL KEEP SLAPPING YOU IN THE FACE!

PAY ATTENTION TO WHAT YOU ARE HEARING.

YOU MAY FIND, THAT YOU COULD HAVE PREVENTED PERSONAL AND CAREER DISASTERS.

YOU MIGHT HAVE IF YOU HAD JUST LISTENED AND READ BETWEEN THE LINES.

BY LISTENING, YOU CAN LEARN WHO MAKES THE DECISIONS OR WHO "WEARS THE PANTS"!

IF A FOREIGN COUNTRY IS SHOUTING "PEACE," BUT IS BUILDING UP ITS ARMY, WHAT DOES YOUR COMMON SENSE TELL YOU?

IF YOUR SPOUSE IS CONSTANTLY COMING HOME LATE OR ALWAYS HAS A HEADACHE, USE YOUR COMMON SENSE!

YOU HAVE TWO EARS

AND ONE MOUTH.

DOES YOUR COMMON

SENSE TELL YOU

ANYTHING?

CHAPTER FIFTEEN   TREATING PEOPLE WITH <u>COMMON SENSE</u> <u>RESPECTFULLY.</u>

<u>SOME OF THIS IS IN 101</u>, BUT YOU MAY HAVE TO LIVE WITH YOUR DECISION FOR THE REST OF YOUR LIFE. IT IS THAT IMPORTANT!

WHY IS IT IMPORTANT TO USE COMMON SENSE IN YOUR TREATING PEOPLE?

YOUR FRIENDS, RELATIVES, AND EVEN BUSINESS ASSOCIATES <u>CANNOT READ YOUR MIND.</u> THEY ONLY KNOW <u>WHAT COMES OUT OF YOUR MOUTH!</u>

SPEAK WITHOUT ACCUSING!

ANSWER WITHOUT ARGUING!

DON'T RAISE YOUR VOICE!

IF YOU ARE MAD ABOUT SOMETHING ELSE; YOUR FAMILY AND FRIENDS <u>WILL THINK YOU ARE MAD AT THEM</u>, IF <u>YOU RAISE YOUR VOICE!</u>

<u>COMMON SENSE MUST BE USED</u> IN DETERMINING FRIENDS,

SPOUSES AND LONG TERM EMPLOYEE/EMPLOYERS AND HOW YOU TREAT THEM.

COMMON SENSE RIGHTNESS: "RIGHT" ALL THE TIME IS "WRONG", FOR ALL SUCCESSFUL RELATIONSHIPS.

IT IS IMPERATIVE THAT ALL PARTIES REALIZE THAT BEING RIGHT ALL THE TIME, IS A DISASTER EVEN IF YOU ARE RIGHT!

SAVE YOUR ENERGY FOR TOPICS THAT ARE IMPORTANT!

DON'T WASTE TIME AND RISK LOSS OF FRIENDSHIP OVER WHO IS RIGHT ON TRIVIAL, MEANINGLESS TOPICS.

WHY DOES COMMON SENSE SAY: EVERYONE SHOULD WORK AND MEET THE PUBLIC BEFORE GRADUATING?

EVERYTHING IS NOT ABSORBED IN SCHOOL, ESPECIALLY COMMON SENSE RESPECTFUL MANNER OF TREATING PEOPLE.

PEOPLE LEARN REAL WORLD LESSONS BY SERVING THE PUBLIC.

PLEASING REAL PEOPLE IS NOT TAUGHT IN STRUCTURED SCHOOL ACTIVITIES!

STUDENTS REMEMBER HOW THEY WERE TREATED.   THEY LEARN HOW TO REACT POSITIVELY BY SERVING THE PUBLIC!

NOTHING TEACHES BETTER THAN COMMON SENSE EXPERIENCE!

HOW THE PUBLIC TREATS STUDENTS, (BAD AND GOOD), IS HOW THEY LEARN TO TREAT AND RESPECT OTHERS.

DON'T FORGET YOUR PROMISES!

EVEN SMALL ONES, "LIKE I WILL TAKE THE BOYS FISHING TOMORROW," ARE IMPORTANT.

IT IS BETTER TO **UNDER PROMISE,** AND **OVER-DELIVER!** PROMISE THEM HAMBURGER, AND GIVE THEM STEAK! THEY WILL REMEMBER IT ALWAYS.

WHAT ARE THE "MUST HAVE" TRAITS FOR SUCCESSFUL RELATIONSHIPS?

HONESTY, EMOTIONAL STABILITY, POSITIVE ATTITUDE, AND THE GOLDEN RULE EMPATHY FOR OTHER PEOPLE!

WHY ARE THESE ATTRIBUTES IMPORTANT?

THE WRONG PERSON CAN INFLUENCE ANYONE!!

BESIDES ALCOHOL AND DRUGS, MOST PEOPLE GET INTO SERIOUS TROUBLE BECAUSE THEY ARE ASSOCIATING WITH THE WRONG CROWD. (USUALLY OLDER)

THAT IS WHEN SOMETHING ILLEGAL HAPPENS!

YOU ARE ONLY AS GOOD OR BAD AS THE PEOPLE BY WHICH YOU ARE SURROUNDED! **YOU ARE WHO YOU ARE SEEN WITH!**

IF YOU RUN WITH DOGS, YOU WILL GET FLEAS.

YOU CAN PUT LIPSTICK ON A PIG, BUT IT IS STILL A PIG!

HOW CAN YOU USE COMMON SENSE TO HELP DETERMINE GOOD RELATIONSHIPS?

IF THEY DO NOT HAVE AT LEAST HALF OF THE ABOVE QUALITIES AND THE WILL TO OBTAIN THE OTHER HALF, THE CHANCES ARE NOT GOOD.

THE NUT DOES NOT FALL FAR FROM THE TREE.

TO IMPROVE YOUR MEMORY, LOAN SOMEONE MONEY!

IF YOU CAN'T FIGURE OUT WHO IS BENEFITING IN ANY RELATIONSHIP; IT'S NOT YOU!

WHAT IS THE SECRET THAT MUST BE LEARNED BEFORE GOING INTO BUSINESS, OR GETTING MARRIED, **THAT 98 PERCENT OF PEOPLE DON'T KNOW?**

IF YOU EXPECT TO HAVE A SUCCESSFUL REWARDING *RELATIONSHIP, YOU HAVE TO START WITH SELECTING THE RIGHT PERSON.*

BEFORE GETTING MARRIED, RUN A CREDIT REPORT ON YOUR FUTURE SPOUSE.

WHY ARE SOME PEOPLE MORE SUCCESSFUL WITH THE OPPOSITE SEX THAN OTHERS?

THEY ASK!

WHY DO SOME PEOPLE ALWAYS GET WHAT THEY WANT?

THEY ASK!

IF YOU THINK THAT MARRIAGE WILL BE ALL BLISS AND HARMONY, LOOK AT YOU AND YOUR SPOUSE'S PARENTS.

IF YOU DON'T HAVE SHARED VALUES, MOST LIKELY, DIVORCE AND FAILURE ARE IN STORE.

SELECT THE RIGHT PEOPLE!

COMMON SENSE

EXPERIENCE

IS THE WORLDS

BEST TEACHER

OF ANY SUBJECT

AT ANY AGE.

JIM MORROW

COMMON SENSE 102
CHAPTER SIXTEEN   "WALK A MILE IN MY SHOES."

FOR SOME REASON, THIS SECRET IS NOT USED BY ENOUGH PEOPLE; IT SHOULD BE 101, BUT AMAZINGLY MOST PEOPLE DO NOT PRACTICE IT.

DO NOT KNEE-JERK TO ANY SITUATION! NO ONE IS COMPLETELY "RIGHT" OR COMPLETELY "WRONG".

HOW A PERSON ACTS USUALLY DEPENDS UPON THEIR CIRCUMSTANCES AT THE MOMENT.

THEY COULD HAVE A HEADACHE, HAVE FINANCIAL TROUBLE, BE SICK, ETC.

WHAT SHOULD YOU DO, IF YOU THINK SOMEONE IS ACTING UNUSUAL TOWARDS YOU, OR ANY SITUATION?

PUT YOURSELF IN THEIR SITUATION. TRY TO DETERMINE WHY THE OTHER PARTY'S OPINION IS DIFFERENT FROM YOURS.

LOOK AT THEIR VIEW OBJECTIVELY.

 IF IT MAKES SENSE, YOU MAY WANT TO CHANGE YOUR VIEW, IF NOT, YOU CAN AT LEAST SEE WHY THE OTHER PARTY FEELS THIS WAY.

YOU CAN EITHER AVOID A CONFLICT, AND BYPASS THE ISSUE, OR HAVE A BETTER INSIGHT INTO HOW TO RESOLVE THE SITUATION.

WHAT IF I STILL THINK THEIR THOUGHTS OR ACTIONS ARE WRONG?

DO NOT ASSUME THAT JUST BECAUSE SOMEONE'S VIEW IS DIFFERENT FROM YOURS, THAT IT IS WRONG.

WHAT IS THE BEST WAY TO REMEMBER THIS BASIC COMMON SENSE SECRET?

MAKE AN EFFORT TO PUT YOURSELF IN ANOTHER'S SHOES AS OFTEN AS POSSIBLE UNTIL IT BECOMES AN AUTOMATIC RESPONSE!

WHEN IT IS AN AUTOMATIC RESPONSE, ANY SITUATION WITH YOUR PERSONAL LIFE OR BUSINESS WILL BECOME EASIER!

I CALL THIS "MUSCLE MEMORY OF THE MIND": THE MORE YOU DO IT, THE MORE AUTOMATIC IT BECOMES.

DO YOU THINK THAT YOU OR YOUR VIEW IS THE ONLY ONE THAT COUNTS?

PUT YOUR FINGER IN A GLASS OF WATER; PULL IT OUT, AND LOOK AT THE BIG HOLE YOU MADE!

COMMON SENSE 102
CHAPTER SEVENTEEN   COMMON SENSE <u>COMPROMISING</u>

WHAT IS COMPROMISING?

IT IS GIVING A LITTLE, TAKE A LITTLE-<u>NO ONE LIKES PEOPLE</u> <u>THAT HAVE TO HAVE THEIR WAY ALL THE TIME.</u>

MOST PROBLEMS NEVER GET SOLVED IF ONE ALWAYS TAKES.

<u>"LIFE IS A NEVER-ENDING TWO-WAY STREET.</u> <u>IT GOES BOTH WAYS.</u>

WHY IS COMPROMISING IMPORTANT?

<u>COMPROMISING IS THE ONLY PEACEFUL WAY THAT WARS, AND</u> <u>EVEN FIGHTS BETWEEN SPOUSES, ARE PREVENTED!</u>

COMPROMISING IS ONLY BASIC COMMON SENSE!

WHAT SHOULD YOU ALWAYS REMEMBER WHEN COMPROMISING?

TRUST YOURSELF, BUT <u>TRY TO UNDERSTAND OTHER POINTS OF</u> <u>VIEW.</u>

FIRST IMPRESSIONS ARE ALMOST ALWAYS RIGHT!

PEOPLE CAN TELL RIGHT OFF THE BAT IF YOU BELIEVE IN WHAT YOU SAY!

BE FRANK, BUT TACTFUL, USE THE GOLDEN RULE AND "WALK A MILE IN MY SHOES' AS YOUR GUIDE IN ANY SITUATION.

AT WHAT POINT DO YOU STOP COMPROMISING?

HAVE A PRE-DETERMINED IDEA ON HOW FAR YOU WILL COMPROMISE, AND WHERE YOU WOULD GO NO FURTHER.

BE PREPARED TO STOP AT THIS POINT AND STICK TO YOUR GUNS.

IF THE OTHER PARTY SENSES THAT YOU ARE WAVERING, YOU WILL BE OUT-NEGOTIATED.

BE PREPARED!

COMMON SENSE WILL TELL YOU THAT AT SOME POINT IN OUR LIVES WE WILL NOT BE ABLE TO NEGOTIATE.

AT SOME POINT, WE CAN'T NEGOTIATE WITH PEOPLE WHO THREAT AND TERRORIZE WITHIN AND OUT OF OUR COUNTRY!

SOME OF OUR LEADERS ARE <u>WOEFULLY ABSENT</u> IN THIS AREA OF <u>COMMON SENSE!</u>

IF WE <u>DO NOT STAND UP</u> AT THIS TIME <u>WE NEVER WILL!</u>

<u>K.I.S.S.</u>

<u>THE EASIEST,</u>

<u>SIMPLEST WAY,</u>

<u>TO COMPROMISE!</u>

BASIC COMMON SENSE 102

CHAPTER EIGHTEEN

BE PREPARED, OOOPS TIME, WORSE CASE SCENARIO-102

SOME OF THIS WAS <u>COVERED IN 101</u>.

BUT LEARNING HOW TO USE THESE SECRETS CAN <u>HELP YOU</u> TO KEEP FRIENDS AND <u>BUSINESS ASSOCIATES</u>, AND TO <u>BE ABLE</u> TO <u>HANDLE ADULT CRISES.</u>

IN WORSE CASE SCENARIOS, IT COULD BE A MATTER OF LIFE OR DEATH!

THIS IS WHY IT IS BEING REPEATED HERE. <u>IF IT SAVES ONE PERSON A LIFETIME OF MISERY, IT IS WORTH REPEATING!</u>

WHAT ARE THE THREE SECRETS THAT CAN HAVE YOU READY FOR ANY EVENTUALITY IN THESE UNCERTAIN TIMES?

BE PREPARED, "OOOPS" TIME, AND WORST CASE SCENARIO!

WHAT ARE THE BEST REASONS TO ALWAYS BE PREPARED?

A SURE-FIRED PRESCRIPTION <u>FOR FAILURE IS NOT BEING</u>

PREPARED! YOU CAN LIVE THROUGH ANYTHING IF YOU ARE PREPARED!

WHAT GOES AROUND, COMES AROUND, <u>SO BE PREPARED TO SHIFT GEARS AT ANY TIME.</u>

<u>EVERYTHING IS ALWAYS CHANGING, NOTHING STAYS THE SAME, BE PREPARED!</u>

YOU CAN'T PRACTICE THINGS THAT HAVE TO BE DONE RIGHT THE FIRST TIME!

<u>WHAT DO YOU DO IF YOU ARE CAUGHT UNPREPARED?</u>

ALWAYS HAVE A PLAN "B".

WHAT IS "OOOPS TIME' AND WHY IS IT IMPORTANT?

"OOOPS TIME" IS ALLOWING TIME TO PREVENT; "OOOPS, SOMETHING WENT WRONG!"

<u>REMEMBER MURPHY'S LAW; IF IT CAN GO WRONG, IT WILL!"</u>

LEAVE PLENTY OF "OOOPS" TIME TO COVER MURPHY'S LAW!

ALWAYS LEAVE YOURSELF PLENTY OF "OOOPS" TIME. IF THE WEDDING IS <u>ON SUNDAY, DON'T WAIT TILL SATURDAY TO SEE IF YOUR TUX FITS!</u>

IF THE BIGGEST CONTRACT OF YOUR LIFE IS TO BE SIGNED AT TWO O'CLOCK, BE THERE AT ONE. <u>NEVER LEAVE TILL TOMORROW WHAT YOU CAN DO TODAY.</u>

WHAT IS "WORST CASE SCENARIO" COMMON SENSE SECRET?

LOOK AT ANY PENDING SITUATION.

BE PREPARED TO HANDLE THE WORST THING THAT CAN HAPPEN WITHOUT SIGNIFICANT DAMAGE IN <u>A "WORSE CASE SCENARIO".</u> THAT IS THE COMMON SENSE SECRET!

IF YOU DO NOT THINK YOU CAN HANDLE THE WORSE THING THAT CAN POSSIBLY HAPPEN, IF YOU DO A CERTAIN THING;

<u>USE YOUR COMMON SENSE! DO NOT DO IT.   SOME THINGS COULD BE FATAL!</u>

IF YOU CAN HANDLE THE CONSEQUENCES OF WHAT MIGHT HAPPEN IN THE WORST CASE SCENARIO, GO AHEAD… <u>IF NOT,</u>

<u>WHEN IN DOUBT…..DON'T!</u>

CHAPTER NINETEEN

TEST BEFORE JUMPING IN!

WHY IS TESTING OR PILOT PROGRAMS COMMON SENSE?

BILLIONS COULD BE SAVED, IF OUR GOVERNMENT <u>WOULD TEST</u> NEW PROGRAMS WITH <u>PILOT PROGRAMS,</u> BEFORE WASTING BILLIONS, <u>AND FIND OUT THAT THEY HARDLY EVER WORK!</u>

BEFORE INVESTING MONEY, YOUR TIME, OR YOUR FEELINGS, IT <u>IS ABSOLUTELY VITAL FOR GOVERNMENTS OR INDIVIDUALS TO TEST!</u>

IT'S TOO LATE TO LOCK THE BARN DOOR AFTER THE HORSE GETS OUT.

HOW DOES IT APPLY PERSONALLY?

TEST YOUR TALK ON A FRIEND BEFORE ASKING FOR A DATE!   IF THEY RESPOND POSITIVELY, GREAT.

<u>IF NOT, YOU CAN FIND OUT WHY, AND CHANGE YOUR TUNE,</u> <u>BEFORE ASKING FOR REAL.</u>

SPEND TIME AND SEE IF YOU ARE COMPATIBLE AND ENJOY THE SAME THINGS BEFORE YOU GET MARRIED.

HAVE YOU EVER BOUGHT A LOT OF NEW THINGS BECAUSE THEY WERE ON SALE?

DID YOU FIND OUT WHEN YOU GOT HOME THAT YOU COULDN'T STAND EVEN ONE OF THEM?

HOW CAN YOU PREVENT THIS KIND OF MISTAKE?

<u>GET ONLY ONE, TO SEE IF YOU REALLY LIKE IT!</u>

YOU CAN ALWAYS GO BACK LATER, THEY HAVE SALES ALL THE TIME!

TEST THE MILK BEFORE YOU BUY THE COW!

<u>THE FEDERAL GOVERNMENT NEVER TESTS TO SEE IF A NEW PROGRAM WORKS.</u>

IT IS NECESSARY THAT ANY PROGRAM BE TESTED TO SEE IF IT WORKS AND <u>IF IT IS GOOD OUR COUNTRY!</u>

WE MUST SET UP A SMALLER TEST BEFORE GOING "FULL-BLOWN;" IN CASE THE PROGRAM IS A FAILURE.

<u>IT IS COMMON SENSE</u> THAT IF THE SMALL TEST IS A FAILURE, IT

WILL NOT BE CATASTROPHIC.

IT WILL SAVE THE GOVERNMENT A LOT OF MONEY AND OUR PEOPLE A LOT OF HEARTACHE!

BEFORE YOU MAKE ANY IMPORTANT DECISION, TEST THE WATER; IF IT SMELLS BAD, DON'T DRINK IT!

COMMON SENSE 102

CHAPTER TWENTY

"GET THE MONEY", SEAL THE DEAL.

SEAL THE DEAL WITH MONEY, OR SOME PHYSICAL EXPRESSION OF THE OTHER PARTY LIVING UP TO YOUR AGREEMENT.

WHY IS 'GET THE MONEY' OR "SEAL THE DEAL", A BASIC COMMON SENSE SECRET THAT PEOPLE MUST KNOW ABOUT?

IT IS TOO EASY FOR THE OTHER PARTY TO HAVE "BUYERS REMORSE," AND CHANGE THEIR MIND IF YOU DON'T!

MOST COMMONLY, "GET THE MONEY," IS ASSOCIATED WITH SELLING SOMETHING.

"GET THE MONEY," IS THE BEST WAY TO KEEP THE SALE CLOSED, AND ASSURING THE OTHER PARTY WILL LIVE UP TO THE DEAL.

BUYER'S REMORSE WILL AFFECT PERSONAL RELATIONSHIPS AS WELL AS SALES! (BUYERS REMORSE IS REGRETTING A PURCHASE)

IF YOU DON'T "GET THE MONEY" AND SEAL THE DEAL; THE PROSPECT WILL GET COLD FEET AND CANCEL THE DEAL.

IN PERSONAL AGREEMENTS, SOME "DEALS" ARE SEALED WITH A GOING STEADY, OR ENGAGEMENT RING.

IT CAN BE A PUBLIC ANNOUNCEMENT, OR ANYTHING THAT LETS THE PUBLIC KNOW OF YOUR AGREEMENT.

IT IS UNLIKELY THAT THE PARTY WILL CHANGE THEIR MIND, AND IT WILL SUFFICE AS "GET THE MONEY".

IN ANY AGREEMENT, "GET THE MONEY" OR "SEAL THE DEAL" BY SOMETHING THAT SHOWS A MEETING OF THE MINDS OF BOTH PARTIES.

COMMON SENSE BUSINESS TIPS

WHAT HAS TO BE DONE BEFORE MOST ANYTHING CAN BE SOLD, INCLUDING SELLING YOURSELF?

YOU CAN BE THE SMARTEST, HAVE THE BEST PRODUCT IN THE WORLD BUT <u>WILL FAIL</u> IF YOU DON'T LET <u>PEOPLE KNOW WHO YOU ARE</u> OR <u>WHAT YOU HAVE TO OFFER!</u>

WHAT DID EVE DO THAT EVERY SUCCESSFUL PERSON NEEDS TO DO TODAY?

SHE USED <u>COMMON SENSE</u> AND <u>ADVERTISED</u>!

WHERE WOULD WE BE IF EVE HADN'T SHOWED ADAM THE APPLE?

NO ONE WOULD EVER KNOW WHAT WE HAVE,

(PERSONALLY OR IN BUSINESS).

WE WILL NEVER SELL ANYTHING, INCLUDING OURSELVES, (EXCEPT TO YOUR RELATIVES), <u>UNLESS WE SHOW THEM WHAT WE HAVE!</u>

WHY HAVE MOST PEOPLE OVER 50 NOT REACHED THE GOALS THEY SET?

THEY DID NOT HAVE A 'PLAN B" TO FALL BACK ON IN CASE THEY FAILED WITH THE FIRST ONE.

WHY MUST YOU DEVELOP A PLAN "B" BEFORE YOU GO TO BED *TONIGHT?*

IT'S TOO LATE TO LOCK THE BARN DOOR AFTER THE HORSE GETS OUT.

WOULD YOU HAVE EVER THOUGHT WE WOULD IN THIS FINANCIAL MESS TODAY?

THESE DESPERATE TIMES THAT PUT YOU UP A TREE, AND CAN **MAKE YOU AFRAID TO CLIMB ON A LIMB, WHERE THE REAL FRUIT IS.**

USE THE SECRETS IN "COMMON SENSE 101-102.

 LAY *GROUNDWORK FOR A BETTER PAYING JOB. OR GO INTO BUSINESS IN A SMALL WAY NOW, WHILE YOU HAVE AN INCOME AND ARE NOT STRESSED.*

WHAT IS THE QUICKEST, SAFEST WAY TO GO INTO BUSINESS FOR YOURSELF WITH THE MOST CHANCE OF SUCCESS THAT 99% OF PEOPLE DON'T KNOW?

BUY AN <u>ON-GOING ESTABLISHED BUSINESS</u>!

<u>WHAT ARE THE BASIC COMMON SENSE WAYS TO GET STARTED IN YOUR OWN BUSINESS?</u>

BE BORN WITH A SILVER SPOON IN YOUR MOUTH, OR O.P.M. WHAT DOES O.P.M. MEAN?

<u>O.P.M.-OTHER PEOPLE'S MONEY.</u>

ANYTIME YOU USE O.P.M., YOU HAVE LEVERAGE TO MULTIPLY EARNINGS AND KEEP MORE CASH!

O.P.M.-FIND PARTNER; YOU DO WORK, HE PROVIDES MONEY.

O.P.M.-FIND A MENTOR, USUALLY A RELATIVE.

O.P.M.-FIND AN INVESTMENT CAPITALIST.

O.P.M.-GET EXTRA SPECIAL TERMS ON ANYTHING, ESPECIALLY REAL ESTATE.

<u>WHAT IS ABOUT THE ONLY WAY TO GET STARTED IF YOU DON'T HAVE ANY OF THE ABOVE?</u>

TAKE A FINANCIAL RISK AND MAKE A NICE PROFIT ON WITH THE FOREGOING COMMON SENSE SECRETS.

MAKING FINANCIAL MOVES THAT SOMEWHAT RISKY ARE ABOUT THE ONLY WAYS TO GET STARTED WITHOUT HELP.

THE YOUNGER YOU CAN TAKE RISKS, THE BETTER.

BEFORE TAKING A RISK, YOU MUST ALWAYS GET THE FACTS, KEEP A RESERVE, AND STAY LIQUID ENOUGH TO HANDLE WORST CASE SCENARIO!

DON'T TAKE RISKS IF TOU CAN'T HANDLE WORST CASE SCENARIO!

WHAT IS THE NUMBER ONE FINANCIAL METHOD THAT IS USED WHEN BUYING OR SELLING A BUSINESS?

OWNER FINANCING: MOST BUSINESSES IN THE WORLD, ESPECIALLY SMALL, ARE BOUGHT AND SOLD WITH OWNER FINANCING!

THE FIRST 10 SECONDS ARE THE MOST IMPORTANT OF YOUR LIFE!

YOU MUST MAKE A GOOD IMPRESSION IMMEDIATELY! THERE IS NEVER A SECOND CHANCE TO MAKE A GOOD IMPRESSION.

THIS **COMMON SENSE FACT** IS **OVERLOOKED** ALMOST ALWAYS!

HOW DO YOU MAKE A GOOD FIRST IMPRESSION?

SMILE! LET THE OTHER PERSON KNOW THAT YOU ARE GENUINELY INTERESTED IN WHAT HE HAS TO SAY.

USE "THE GOLDEN RULE". DO UNTO OTHERS, LISTEN TO OTHERS, ASK THEIR OPINIONS.

IF YOU HAVE AN UNCOMFORTABLE FEELING WHEN YOU MEET SOMEONE, EVEN PROSPECTIVE EMPLOYEE/EMPLOYER; OR A SALESMAN THAT **COULDN'T SELL A CAR** OR MINK COAT FOR $5;

THAT PERSON HAS NOT MADE A GOOD FIRST IMPRESSION.

CONVERSELY, LOOK AT THE SALESMAN YOU REALLY LIKE, AND HAS SOLD YOU MANY THINGS OVER THE YEARS.

LOOK AT SOMEONE YOU HIT IT OFF WITH RIGHT AWAY, SOMEONE

THAT PUT YOU AT EASE, AS SOON AS YOU TWO MET.

MOST OF THE TIME THE FIRST 10 SECONDS DETERMINED WHICH WAY THINGS WERE GOING TO TURN OUT!

PE0PLE DECIDE IN TEN SECONDS OR LESS IF THEY LIKE AND WANT TO TAKE THE RELATIONSHIP OR BUSINESS FURTHER!

PRINCETON RESEARCHERS FOUND THAT PEOPLE MAY DECIDE ON YOUR TRUSTWORTHINESS IN AS LITTLE AS **THREE SECONDS.**

A BRITISH STUDY FOUND THAT WOMEN WITH VISIBLE TATTOOS WERE **PERCEIVED AS LESS ATTRACTIVE**, HEAVIER DRINKERS, ETC. THAN WOMEN WITHOUT TATTOOS.

A 2007 UNIVERSITY STUDY FOUND THAT **LOOKING** YOUR CONVERSATION **PARTNER IN THE EYE MIGHT HELP PEOPLE SEE YOU AS MORE INTELLIGENT.**

STUDIES HAVE ALSO SHOWN THAT PEOPLE MAKE UP THEIR MINDS ABOUT **YOUR STATUS** & WEALTH IN SECONDS.

THEY LOOK AT YOUR NEATNESS, HOW YOU ARE DRESSED AND HOW YOU CARRY YOURSELF.

GOOD USE OF

THE FIRST TEN

SECONDS; WILL

MAKE MOST

ANYONE A SUCCESS,

IF PEOPLE

WILL JUST USE

THEM CORRECTLY.

CHAPTER TWENTY-THREE   COMMON SENSE WEIGHT LOSS AND FITNESS SECRETS.

WHY ARE WE FAT? WHAT CAN WE DO?

THERE ARE <u>THREE COMMON SENSE WEIGHT LOSS & FITNESS SOLUTIONS</u>; THEY ARE NOT DIETS, CALORIES, CARBOHYDRATES, AND STARVING!

<u>I WILL SHOW</u> THEM TO YOU, BUT <u>YOU ALONE</u> MUST <u>REALIZE THEY ARE TRUE</u>. <u>YOU</u> MUST <u>DECIDE</u> TO <u>EMBRACE</u> THE THREE SOLUTIONS <u>YOURSELF</u>, NO ONE CAN DO IT FOR YOU.

IF YOU <u>DON'T EMBRACE THEM</u>, YOU MAY AS WELL <u>STOP READING HERE</u>. I CAN'T HELP YOU!

IF YOU USE THESE THREE COMMON SENSE SOLUTIONS, THERE ARE <u>FIVE OTHER THINGS</u> THAT <u>I CAN DO</u> TO <u>HELP YOU</u> LOSE AND <u>GET FIT</u>.

THREE WEIGHT LOSS SOLUTIONS

1. WE MUST MUST SEE THEMSELVES AS OTHERS SEE US! WE DO NOT REALLY PERCEIVE OURSELVES AS WE REALLY ARE. FAT, FAT, FAT FAT!

WHY ARE WE STILL OVERWEIGHT??

BECAUSE WE DO NOT REALLY "SEE" OURSELVES AS OTHERS SEE US.

TAKE YOUR "BEFORE" PICTURE AND PUT IT ON YOUR TABLE, YOUR DESK, AND REFRIGERATOR LIKE I DID MINE. IT REMINDS US DAILY OF HOW FAT WE "REALLY" LOOK!

SEE OURSELVES AS OTHERS SEE US.

I WAS MASSIVELY OBESE FOR ABOUT 50 YEARS, AFTER PLAYING FOOTBALL. I WENT FROM ONE HUNDRED EIGHTY-FIVE POUNDS TO TWO HUNDRED THIRTY POUNDS IN TWO TO THREE YEARS.

I WAS STILL ACTIVE, AND HAD A LARGE BONE STRUCTURE. I WAS OKAY AT THIS WEIGHT. OVER THE NEXT 50 YEARS, I WOULD ADD A FEW POUNDS A EVERY YEAR, BUT IT DID NOT EVEN BOTHER ME.

AS I DEVELOPED SEVERE BACK PROBLEMS, EVERY DOCTOR I WENT TO, WANTED ME TO LOSE WEIGHT.

I WAS BUSY BUILDING A FURNITURE AND REAL ESTATE DEVELOPMENT BUSINESS, AND <u>I DID NOT THINK I HAD ENOUGH OF A WEIGHT PROBLEM TO WORRY ABOUT.</u>

EVEN WHEN I GOT UP TO TWO HUNDRED AND EIGHTY POUNDS, I WAS STILL PLAYING SINGLES TENNIS.

I PLAYED TENNIS UNTIL I WENT WELL OVER THREE HUNDRED POUNDS.

<u>I STILL DID NOT BELIEVE I HAD A SEVERE WEIGHT PROBLEM!</u>

I HAD PLAYED GOLF SINCE I WAS IN COLLEGE, SO WHEN I STARTED HAVING DIFFICULTY PLAYING TENNIS, I GAVE IT UP IN FAVOR OF GOLF; STILL NOT CONCERNED ABOUT MY WEIGHT.

<u>AFTER I RETIRED, I STARTED TO HAVE MORE HEALTH PROBLEMS, AND EVEN HAVE A PACEMAKER.</u>

I SLOWLY BEGAN TO NOTICE THAT THINGS WERE BECOMING MORE DIFFICULT.

AFTER RETIREMENT, I SHOPPED A LITTLE AT WALMART AND <u>NOTICED SOMETHING AMAZING!</u>

I WAS PREVIOUSLY SO BUSY WITH BUSINESS, THAT I HAD <u>TUNNEL VISION, AS TO THE WAY THAT MOST PEOPLE PHYSICALLY</u>

APPEARED. I NOW SAW WHAT I WAS MISSING!

MOST SHOPPERS AT WALMART APPEARED VASTLY OVERWEIGHT!

A LOT OF THEM LOOKED LIKE THEY COULD BARELY WALK. HOW THEY COULD LET THEMSELVES GET IN THAT SHAPE?

AFTER A WHILE, IT SLOWLY SEEPED INTO ME THAT I MAY LOOK OVERWEIGHT ALSO. I REMEMBER A COUPLE OF TIMES <u>ASKING MY WIFE: DO I LOOK AS BIG AS THAT GUY AT THE COUNTER?</u>

SHE WOULD GRACIOUSLY SAY SOMETHING LIKE, I WAS BIG, BUT NOT FLABBY, LIKE THAT.

<u>IT WENT ON UNTIL I GOT SO BIG, (375 POUNDS) THAT I COULD NOT SHOP WALMART, IF THEY DID NOT HAVE A CHAIR I COULD RIDE IN.</u>

MY SPINAL STENOSIS PUT ME IN A WHEELCHAIR, AND I DEVELOPED DIABETES.

THAT'S WHEN I FOUND OUT WHY THAT NINETY-NINE PERCENT OF PEOPLE ARE UNSUCCESSFUL AT LOSING WEIGHT AND GETTING FIT!

ALL OF WEIGHT LOSS AND FITNESS PROGRAMS HAVE ONE THING IN COMMON: THEY HARDLY EVER WORK!

BUT NOW I HAVE FOUND OUT WHY!

PEOPLE DO NOT USE COMMON SENSE AND REALLY PERCEIVE THEMSELVES AS FAT!

MOST PEOPLE ARE JUST LIKE ME. THEY DON'T REALLY SEE THEMSELVES AS BEING TOO FAT, UNTIL IT IS USUALLY TOO LATE!

BY THE TIME WE REALIZE THAT WE HAVE A REAL PROBLEM, WE ARE USUALLY SO BIG OR SO OLD, IT IS ALMOST IMPOSSIBLE TO DO ANYTHING ABOUT IT!

WE RATIONALIZE THAT WE ARE JUST HEAVY AND DON'T HAVE A REAL PROBLEM. EVENTUALLY WE CAN'T DO DAILY TASKS, AND EVEN HAVE TO HAVE FRIENDS AND RELATIVES DO THINGS FOR US!

IT IS USUALLY TOO LATE THEN. WE USUALLY HAVE SO MANY HEALTH PROBLEMS MADE WORSE BY THE WEIGHT, WE COULD NOT DO ANYTHING, UNTIL I DISCOVERED MY FITNESS PROGRAM.

NOW WE CAN DO SOMETHING ABOUT IT, NO MATTER WHAT SHAPE WE ARE IN. I WAS 375 POUNDS IN A WHEELCHAIR. I LOST 150 POUNDS; OUT OF THE CHAIR AND DOING ANYTHING I WANT.

MY COMMON SENSE FITNESS PROGRAM "ISOSTRETCH" IS DISCUSSED IN THE NEXT TWO CHAPTERS.

I BELIEVE THE MAJOR REASON DIET PLANS HARDLY EVER WORK IS BECAUSE WE DON'T BELIEVE WE HAVE A REAL PROBLEM UNTIL IT IS TOO LATE.

ANYONE WITH A DESTRUCTIVE HABIT, SUCH AS OBESITY, ALCOHOL OR DRUG ADDICTION, <u>WILL NOT CHANGE UNTIL THEY HAVE A SEVERE REASON.</u>

NO AMOUNT OF PLEADING AND HELP BY SOMEONE ELSE WILL WORK, UNTIL <u>THIS CRITICAL REASON FORCES THEM TO MAKE UP THEIR OWN MIND TO CHANGE.</u>

WE MUST BEGIN TO BE HONEST, REALIZE THAT WE REALLY HAVE A SERIOUS PROBLEM, <u>AND SEE OURSELVES AS WE REALLY ARE, AND HOW OTHERS ACTUALLY SEE US.</u>

WE WILL <u>NEVER MAKE UP OUR MINDS</u> TO DO <u>THE HARD THINGS</u> THAT IT TAKES TO GET US <u>FIT UNTIL WE DO</u>.

HOWEVER, <u>OBESITY</u> IS AN <u>EPIDEMIC</u> PROBLEM, ESPECIALLY AMONG OUR <u>YOUNG</u> AND <u>ELDERLY</u>.

BY NOT REALLY RECOGNIZING THE PROBLEM LIKE ME, OUR YOUNG PEOPLE MAY GO <u>FOR 20 OR 30 YEARS</u> BEFORE THEY <u>FIGURE OUT THEY HAVE A PROBLEM.</u>

THEY NEED TO RECOGNIZE THE PROBLEM WHILE THEY ARE <u>YOUNG ENOUGH</u> TO DO WHATEVER IS <u>NECESSARY TO CHANGE,</u> WITHOUT HAVING THE <u>ADDITIONAL PROBLEMS THAT AGE BRINGS</u>.

WEIGHT LOSS SOLUTION # 2.

IF YOU HAVE A <u>SERIOUS WEIGHT</u> PROBLEM, LOSING WEIGHT, AND CHANGING YOUR LIFESTYLE ARE THE <u>MOST IMPORTANT THINGS YOU CAN DO,</u> NOT JUST FOR YOURSELF, <u>BUT FOR YOUR FAMILY!!</u>

WE MUST CARE ENOUGH FOR <u>OUR FAMILIES TO REALIZE</u> THAT OUR <u>FAMILY IS DEPENDENT UPON US.</u>

WE CAN'T HELP OUR FAMILIES, IF WE DON'T HELP OUR SELVES FIRST!

AFTER I BECAME DISABLED, MY DISABLED WIFE HAD TO HELP ME DO SOME THINGS.

I REALIZED THAT THE <u>MOST IMPORTANT</u> THING <u>IN MY LIFE</u> SHOULD BE TAKING CARE OF MY <u>PHYSICAL</u> AND <u>MENTAL CONDITION.</u>

<u>IF NOT, I WOULD BE BURDENING MY FAMILY, RATHER THAN TAKING CARE OF THEM.</u>

<u>IT WAS COMMON SENSE!</u> I COULD NOT DO WHAT IS BEST FOR MY

FAMILY, IF I DID NOT <u>TAKE CARE OF MYSELF FIRST.</u>

FOR THE SERIOUSLY OBESE LIKE I WAS; ALCOHOLICS, OR DRUG ADDICTS; <u>IT IS IMPERATIVE THAT THEY REALIZE THIS AND ACT ACCORDINGLY.</u>

IF THEY DON'T, THEY WON'T BE IN THIS WORLD MUCH LONGER, <u>OR WORSE, THEY WILL BE AN INVALID BURDENING THEIR FAMILY!</u>

ONCE THEY REALIZE THIS, THEY MAY MAKE UP THEIR MINDS TO DO IT, <u>IF THEY REALLY CARE FOR THEIR FAMILY.</u>

IF THEY CONTINUE WITH THEIR DESTRUCTIVE AND <u>SELFISH</u> *BEHAVIOR, <u>RELATIVES AND FRIENDS SHOULD ADOPT A TOUGH LOVE APPROACH!</u>*

OTHERWISE, <u>FAMILIES AND FRIENDS</u> WILL BECOME <u>ENABLERS</u>, AND <u>THE PERSON WILL NEVER CHANGE.</u> IF YOU CONTINUE TO <u>ENABLE THEM</u>, <u>THEY WILL USE YOU</u>, BUT REALLY <u>WILL CARE LESS ABOUT YOU.</u>

WEIGHT LOSS SOLUTION # 3.

WE MUST HAVE AN <u>INCENTIVE</u> TO LOSE WEIGHT.

MY <u>INCENTIVE</u> WAS <u>REALIZING</u> THAT IF I DID NOT, I WOULD BE <u>BURDENING MY FAMILY</u> FOR YEARS, AND END UP IN A NURSING HOME WAY BEFORE MY TIME!

I HAD ALSO JUST SHOWN TO BE <u>DIABETIC</u>; WHICH I HAD SUSPECTED FOR SOME TIME.

<u>YOUR INCENTIVE</u> CAN BE A NEW WARDROBE, SCHOOL REUNION, GOING TO THE BEACH FOR THE FIRST TIME IN YEARS, OR SOMETHING FRIVOLOUS LIKE THAT.

THAT MAY WORK FOR A <u>LITTLE BIT</u>; BUT IF YOU REALLY NEED TO LOSE WEIGHT, YOU NEED A <u>SERIOUS INCENTIVE</u>.

ONE TO BE <u>CONSIDERED</u> MOST, IS <u>YOUR</u> AND YOUR <u>FAMILY'S</u> <u>HEALTH</u>. YOU NEED TO <u>REALIZE</u> WHAT A <u>BURDEN</u> YOUR WEIGHT CAN BE ON <u>YOUR FAMILY</u>.

EVERYONE HAS TO <u>MAKE UP THEIR OWN MIND</u>. THE ONLY WAY <u>THAT ANYONE CAN HELP</u> AN OBESE PERSON, A DRUG ADDICT OR ALCOHOLIC, IS TO <u>GIVE THEM AN INCENTIVE</u> IF THEY WON'T FIND ONE FOR THEMSELVES.

IT MAY BE SOMETHING AS <u>DRASTIC</u> AS "IF YOU STOP DRINKING," I WILL NOT GET A DIVORCE, OR SOMETHING AS <u>SERIOUS</u>.

IF YOU HAVE A SERIOUS PROBLEM, IT IS BETTER THAT YOU

HAVE **YOUR OWN INCENTIVE** THAN HAVE **SOMEONE MAKE ONE FOR YOU.**

IF YOU DO NOT ADDRESS THE THREE ABOVE WEIGHT LOSS SOLUTIONS OF; **SEEING YOURSELF** AS SEEN BY **OTHERS**, MAKE LOSING WEIGHT THE MOST **IMPORTANT THING** IN YOUR LIFE, AND HAVE A **STRONG INCENTIVE**; I CANNOT HELP YOU.

IF YOU DO ADDRESS THE ABOVE, THERE ARE FIVE THINGS I CAN DO TO HELP!

1. WE MUST USE **COMMON SENSE EATING!**

WE GET TIRED, BORED AND HUNGRY WITH DIETS AND THEIR RABBIT FOOD.

THE BEST WAY TO DIET IS TO EAT FOODS YOU LIKE, USE SMALLER PORTIONS, EAT SLOWLY AND SAVOR EVERY BITE.

USE **COMMON SENSE!** EAT WHAT **YOU ENJOY!** EAT A FRESH **BANANA** INSTEAD OF BANANA **PUDDING.**

CHEW YOUR FOOD <u>THIRTY TIMES</u> BEFORE SWALLOWING.

<u>THE ENZYMES</u> IN YOUR <u>SALIVA</u> HELP DIGESTION AND MAKE YOU <u>FEEL FULL</u>.

<u>YOUR BODY DOES NOT HAVE AS MUCH TIME TO ABSORB THE FAT!</u>

DO NOT EAT ANYTHING AFTER SIX AT NIGHT UNLESS IT HAS ALMOST NO BAD CARBS. ISOSTRETCH BEFORE YOU GO TO BED IF YOU CAN. IT WILL HELP YOU SLEEP.

STUDIES SHOW THAT YOU HAVE AN AFTER BURN OF CALORIES AFTER EXERCISING, ESPECIALLY IN YOUR SLEEP.

WHY IS IT <u>COMMON SENSE</u> THAT THE <u>LONGER YOU SLEEP</u>, THE MORE WEIGHT YOU WILL LOSE? <u>YOU CAN'T EAT IF YOU ARE ASLEEP! I HAVE PROVED IT WORKS.</u>

SEE MY TIPS ON HYDRATION AND DIET DRINKS IN MY BOOK "ISOSTRETCH".

<u>LEARN GOOD CARBS FROM BAD CARBS</u>, BUT PRIMARILY, EAT <u>SMALLER AMOUNTS</u> AND <u>ISOSTRETCH DAILY</u>.

MY <u>DAILY EATING RECORD</u> KEEPS YOU ON TRACK: IT SHOWS YOU WHAT YOU ARE "<u>REALLY</u>" DOING EACH DAY.

EAT FRUITS AND VEGETABLES FOR REGULARITY, AND OTHER COMMON SENSE EATING TECHNIQUES.

<u>AVOID HUNGER ATTACKS</u>. USE COMMON SENSE BY SNACKING ONLY WITH <u>LOW CARB</u> FOODS.

<u>WATER</u> IS THE MOST <u>"ANTI-AGING" FOOD</u> IN OUR LIVES.

2. WE MUST DO SOME TYPE OF EXERCISE, IF IT IS ONLY ROLLING AROUND IN BED!

I FOUND THE EXERCISES THAT ALMOST ANYONE CAN DO WITH MY DISCOVERY OF "ISOSTRETCH." I WROTE AN EARLIER BOOK BASED ON MY WEIGHT LOSS EXPERIENCE THAT <u>CAN HELP MILLIONS OF PEOPLE</u>. SEE THE NEXT CHAPTERS.

I WROTE THE BOOK FOR PEOPLE THAT HAVE STRUGGLED WITH WEIGHT, LIKE I HAVE; OR EVEN ALCOHOL AND DRUG PROBLEMS.

I ESPECIALLY WANT TO HELP PEOPLE THAT HAVE TRIED, AND FAILED DOING ANYTHING ABOUT THEIR PROBLEMS.

<u>I KNOW HOW HARD IT IS!</u>

IN MY EARLIER "ISOSTRETCH" BOOK, THERE ARE COMMON SENSE TIPS ON EVERYTHING, INCLUDING HOW I LOST WEIGHT AND GOT FIT. THERE IS A CONDENSATION OF IT IN THIS BOOK.

WE DON'T EXERCISE SOMETIMES BECAUSE IT IS PAINFUL OR TOO STRENUOUS.

"ISOSTRETCH" ENABLES PEOPLE WHO WERE PREVIOUSLY UNABLE OR UNWILLING TO DO REGULAR EXERCISE.

THEY CAN EXERCISE ON THEIR BED OR CHAIR, WITH NO PAIN OR STRAIN, AS I DID DURING MY 150 POUND WEIGHT LOSS.

ISOSTRETCH IS A "NO SWEAT" FITNESS PLAN OF ISOMETRICS AND STRETCHING.

IT IS RECOMMENDED BY DOCTOR PERRY SAVAGE. HE IS FOUNDER OF ALABAMA ORTHOPEDIC SPINE AND SPORTS MEDICINE ASSOCIATES.

THE AMERICAN HEART ASSOCIATION'S STUDY, PUBLISHED IN FEBRUARY 2013, A YEAR AFTER MY ISOSTRETCH DISCOVERY IN MARCH OF 2012, SAID, QUOTE:

"THIS STUDY DEMONSTRATED THAT ISOMETRIC

HAND GRIP TRAINING, AND ISOMETRIC LEG TRAINING, RESULTED <u>IN LARGER REDUCTIONS IN SYSTOLIC BLOOD PRESSURE.....</u>"

A <u>GREAT TESTAMENT</u> FOR MY <u>ISOSTRETCH PLAN!</u>

I FOUND THAT <u>MY EXERCISES</u> WERE LOWERING MY <u>BLOOD</u> <u>PRESSURE, A</u> <u>YEAR BEFORE</u> THE HEART ASSOCIATION'S <u>STUDY CAME OUT!</u>

ISOSTRETCH IS FUN AND EASY; IF IT HURTS, STOP AND DO LESS!

<u>THIS ANTI-AGING, NON-STRENUOUS FITNESS PLAN,</u> IS FOR EVERYONE REGARDLESS OF AGE OR PHYSICAL ABILITY.

IT HAS EATING TIPS AND SECRETS THAT SMASH HUNGER ATTACKS.

<u>THIS INEXPENSIVE PLAN IS FOR EVERYONE,</u> BUT ESPECIALLY FOR ONES UNABLE TO DO REGULAR EXERCISE.

<u>IT EVEN TEACHES CHILDREN A STRUCTURED METHOD</u> FOR HANDLING FITNESS AS WELL AND OTHER DIFFICULT TASKS THAT LIE AHEAD.

HARD WORK WAS THE EXERCISE AND STRUCTURE THAT OUR

PARENTS TAUGHT US YEARS AGO!

TODAY, MOST PEOPLE'S ONLY EXERCISE IS WITH THEIR FINGERS OR THUMB ON CELL PHONES OR COMPUTERS!

MOST CHILDREN REGARD ISOSTRETCHES AS FUN.

THERE IS A BETTER CHANCE OF THEM LEARNING ISOSTRETCH, OF THAN THEM LEARNING MUSIC.

3. WE MUST AND CAN MAKE THE TIME.

LEARN HOW THE BUSY MAKE TIME! THE SECRET TO THE PROBLEM OF "WE DON'T HAVE TIME" IS: WRITE IT DOWN!

BY WRITING IT DOWN, YOU **AUTOMATICALLY REMEMBER** WHAT **AND WHEN YOU MUST DO** THINGS.

YOU ARE PROMPTED TO DO THINGS AUTOMATICALLY. THINGS **DO NOT GET TIED UP, DELAYED, OR FORGOTTEN ALTOGETHER.**

IT'S AUTOMATIC! IT SAVES A LOT OF TIME AND GIVES YOU THE TIME TO ACCOMPLISH EVERYTHING YOU NEED TO DO. LIKE EXERCISING!

REFRESH YOURSELF WITH THE PREVIOUS CHAPTERS ON "WRITE IT DOWN." YOU WILL NOTICE THE <u>IMPORTANCE I PLACE ON WRITING IT DOWN.</u>

ANYONE THAT IS WORKING <u>WILL NOT</u> FIND THE TIME TO LOSE WEIGHT, IF THEY <u>DO NOT WRITE</u> THINGS <u>DOWN.</u> EVEN IF YOU ARE RETIRED LIKE ME, YOU WILL SKIP EXERCISING DAY BY DAY, <u>UNTIL YOU DO NOT DO IT ALL</u>, IF YOU DON'T STAY IN <u>THE HABIT OF WRITING IT DOWN.</u>

THE COMMON SENSE SECRETS SHOWN ABOVE ARE THINGS THAT WE WILL ALL <u>ADMIT</u> TO, AS WHY WE ARE IN TERRIBLE SHAPE.

THERE ARE <u>TWO OTHER THINGS</u> THAT HAVE US IN THIS SHAPE, <u>THAT WE DON'T USUALLY ADMIT TO:</u>

4. <u>WE MUST AND CAN CONTROL OUR WILL POWER.</u>

<u>"MUSCLE MEMORY OF THE MIND"</u> IS AN EASY WAY FOR A HARD-TO-DO SUBJECT; WILL POWER!

IT IS <u>NEEDED</u> TO ACCOMPLISH THE <u>FORMIDABLE TASK</u> OF <u>EATING LESS AND EXERCISING MORE.</u>

BEFORE NOW, WE <u>HAVE NOT HAD</u> THE WILL POWER TO ACCOMPLISH THE TASK OF LOSING WEIGHT, STAYING FIT AND CHANGING LIFESTYLES.

CONTROLLING WILL POWER IS <u>TOO HARD</u> FOR <u>MY CONSCIOUS MIND OR YOURS: IT HAS ENOUGH PROBLEMS.</u>

<u>YOUR SUBCONSCIOUS MUST HELP OUR CONSCIOUS MIND.</u>

YOUR SUBCONSCIOUS MIND DOES THE WORK!

<u>TO DO THIS, I DEVELOPED "MUSCLE MEMORY OF THE MIND."</u>

EXPLAINED EARLIER, IT <u>SUBCONSCIOUSLY HELPS YOUR MIND</u> REACT, AS YOUR <u>LEG MUSCLES REACT</u>, FOR WHAT MUST BE DONE TO <u>KICK A FOOTBALL</u>.

"MUSCLE MEMORY OF THE MIND" IS FURTHER EXPLAINED IN MY BOOK "ISOSTRETCH".

IT IS DEVELOPING A HABIT OF DOING WHAT IS NECESSARY TO ACHIEVE YOUR GOALS DAILY; THEN LETTING MUSCLE MEMORY OF YOUR MIND TAKE OVER!

MY SUBCONSCIOUS <u>CONTROLS MY WILL POWER</u> AND ENABLES ME TO STAY ON THE ISOSTRETCH PROGRAM.

5. WE MUST KNOW HOW TO GET OVER <u>PLATEAUS</u>. (TIMES WHEN YOU DON'T SEEM TO BE IMPROVING)

I WENT ALONG ABOUT THREE MONTHS, LOSING ABOUT 10 POUNDS A MONTH.

THEN I DID WHAT <u>EVERYONE DOES</u> THAT HAS EVER TRIED TO LOSE WEIGHT. I WENT FOR <u>TWO WEEKS NOT LOSING A POUND.</u>

IT <u>HAPPENS ON EVERY WEIGHT LOSS PROGRAM!</u> THAT IS THE <u>MAJOR REASON</u> WEIGHT LOSS <u>PROGRAMS DO NOT WORK</u>!

WHEN PEOPLE HAVE STRUGGLED SO HARD, AND HAVE EATEN NOTHING BUT RABBIT FOOD<u>, THEY USUALLY DROP THE PROGRAM.   THEY COULD NOT SEE ANY IMPROVEMENT</u>!

THE ONLY MEASUREMENT OF THEIR IMPROVING WAS THE <u>WEIGHT SCALE.</u>

LIKE EVERYONE ELSE, AFTER DOING SO GOOD, BUT NOT LOSING ANYTHING FOR TWO WEEKS, I <u>WAS READY TO QUIT.</u>

HOWEVER, I TRIED ON A NEW PAIR OF PANTS THAT NEEDED A

BELT.

I USUALLY WORE LOOSE FITTING CLOTHES, WITH A FLEXIBLE WAISTLINE.

WHEN I ADJUSTED THE BELT, I FOUND THAT I HAD LOST TWO INCHES IN THE LAST TWO WEEKS!

MY ISOSTRETCH DISCOVERY HAD TIGHTENED UP MY CORE AND GAVE THE CONFIDENCE TO CONTINUE.

TO HELP MYSELF, I DEVELOPED THE FITNESS PROGRAM CALLED "ISOSTRETCH". AFTER PROVING IT HELPED ME, I WROTE THIS BOOK FOR OTHERS.

ISOSTRETCH IS AN EASY, FUN, TONING, ANTI-AGING MELTING OF AN ISOMETRICS AND STRETCHING FITNESS PLAN.

IT HAS EATING TIPS, THAT ALMOST ANYONE, EVEN THE DISABLED CAN DO.

 IT IS PAINLESS AND YOU CAN DO IT ON YOUR BED OR CHAIR!

LIKE ANY SERIOUSLY OBESE PERSON, ALCOHOLIC, OR DRUG ADDICT; TO BE SUCCESSFUL AT ANY REHAB, I HAD TO MAKE UP MY OWN MIND TO DO IT!

I REALIZED THAT I COULD NOT TAKE CARE OF MY FAMILY,

THIS WAS THE INCENTIVE THAT I NEEDED TO MAKE UP MY MIND TO LOSE WEIGHT, AND GET FIT.

<u>I HAD FOUND WHAT WORKED FOR ME!</u>

MY INCENTIVE WAS THE REALIZATION THAT I HAD TO TAKE CARE OF MYSELF FIRST!

<u>I DISCOVERED</u> HOW TO DO WHAT DOCTORS AND OTHERS HAD TRIED TO HELP ME DO, FOR 50 YEARS.

SO, I <u>WROTE THESE BOOKS</u> TO TRY TO <u>HELP OTHERS.</u>   SOME <u>DOCTORS</u> COULD <u>NOT BELIEVE</u> THAT I <u>DID NOT HAVE SURGERY!</u>

COMMON SENSE 102
CHAPTER TWENTY-FOUR

HOW I DID IT, AND HOW YOU CAN.

BEFORE   375 LBS.   AFTER 225 LBS.

I WAS A 375 POUND, 70-YEAR-OLD DISABLED PERSON, WITH A <u>PACEMAKER</u> IN A <u>WHEELCHAIR</u>. I WAS <u>MORBIDLY OBESE</u> WITH <u>SLEEP APNEA</u>.

I HAD SEVERE SPINAL STENOSIS, ARTHRITIS, DIABETES, PULMONARY HYPERTENSION, HEART, PACEMAKER PROBLEMS, DIZZINESS AND BRAIN SURGERY.

<u>I HAD OTHER PROBLEMS AND TEN DOCTORS</u>.

I WAS TAKING 30 PILLS A DAY. I HAD ONE FOOT IN THE GRAVE.

I COULD NOT WALK OVER TEN YARDS.

ANY REGULAR EXERCISE WAS PAINFUL! BEING SEVENTY YEARS OLD IS PAINFUL ENOUGH, BUT BEING FAT AS I WAS, MADE IT UNBEARABLE!

I WAS LIKE MOST PEOPLE THAT ARE GROSSLY OVERWEIGHT.

I WAS NOT HONEST WITH MYSELF!

WHEN I LOOKED IN A MIRROR, I SAW MYSELF AS STOCKY, SOMEWHAT OVERWEIGHT, **NOT MASSIVELY OBESE!**

WHEN I DEVELOPED DIABETES AND MY WIFE HAD TO HELP ME DO SOME THINGS, **I FINALLY DECIDED IT WAS TIME TO LOSE WEIGHT, GET IN SHAPE.**

MY WIFE ALREADY HAD A **STROKE**, BARELY ABLE TO TAKE CARE OF HERSELF.

SHE CERTAINLY **COULD NOT TAKE CARE OF ME.** IN MY SHAPE, I COULD NOT **HELP MYSELF OR HER.**

MY DOCTORS HAD BEEN TRYING TO GET ME TO LOSE WEIGHT FOR YEARS.

THEY ALL TOLD ME THAT THE OLDER I GOT, THE HARDER IT WAS TO LOSE WEIGHT, AND I HAD TRIED WITH NO SUCCESS.

HOWEVER, I KNEW THAT I COULD PARTIALLY ADJUST MY EATING HABITS.

BUT, IN MY SHAPE, **I COULD NOT DO STANDARD TYPES OF EXERCISE, WHICH IS ESSENTIAL TO LOSING WEIGHT AND GETTING FIT.**

I WAS GETTING WORSE DAILY AND KNEW I HAD TO DO **SOMETHING QUICK**, OR I WOULD BE IN A **NURSING HOME!**

I LOST **150 POUNDS**, LOST A **FOOT AND A HALF IN THE WAIST,** GOT OUT OF THE WHEEL CHAIR, AND **CONTROLLED MY DIABETES.**

EVERYONE ASKS ME, HOW DID YOU DO IT?

MY DOCTORS WERE AMAZED! MOST ASKED: DID YOU HAVE SURGERY?

THEY SAID **ANYONE** THAT IS 70 YEARS OLD, **AS FAT** AND OUT OF SHAPE AS I WAS; **DISABLED**, AND **IN PAIN, WOULDN'T GET BETTER WITHOUT SURGERY.**

MY DOCTORS SAID THAT THEY **HAD NEVER SEEN ANYONE IN MY CONDITION, AT MY AGE, COME BACK!**

DOCTORS HAD ALWAYS TOLD ME THE ANSWER TO GETTING FIT AND STAYING THAT WAY IS SIMPLE: EAT LESS AND EXERCISE MORE!

IF IT IS THAT SIMPLE, WHY AREN'T MILLIONS OF OVERWEIGHT PEOPLE GETTING FIT AND STAYING THAT WAY?

THEY DO NOT KNOW WHAT I DISCOVERED.

ISOSTRETCH:

"AMERICAN COMMON SENSE YOGA"

COMMON SENSE 102
CHAPTER TWENTY-FIVE

"ISOSTRETCH; "CALLED AMERICAN COMMON SENSE YOGA: EASY, RELAXING COMBINATION OF ISOMETRICS AND STRETCHING. .

"ISOSTRETCH IS DONE IN A CHAIR OR ON A BED; IT IS SIMPLE, RELAXING MOVEMENTS THAT EVERYONE CAN DO AND ENJOY, EVEN SKINNY FOLKS!

IT IS ESPECIALLY GOOD FOR PEOPLE LIKE ME THAT COULD BARELY WALK!

SLOW AND EASY IS THE KEY. DO ONLY AS MANY AS COMFORTABLE, RELAX. YOU DON'T HAVE TO DO THEM ALL AT ONE TIME.

YOU DON'T EVEN HAVE TO WORRY ABOUT DOING THEM RIGHT OR THE CORRECT NUMBER. THE BODY LOVES CONFUSION!

YOU CAN DO MOST OF THE MOVEMENTS ANYWHERE, ANYTIME OF THE DAY IN A CHAIR! A FEW ENJOYABLE, RELAXING MINUTES HERE, A FEW THERE, ESPECIALLY IF YOU ARE ON A COMPUTER ALL DAY LONG.

FOUR MOVEMENTS CAN BE DONE ON A BED FOR MINUTES

AT <u>NIGHT</u>!

IN THIS COMMON SENSE BOOK, THERE ARE COMMON SENSE TIPS ON EVERYTHING. YOU CAN MAKE UP YOUR MIND IF THE CONDENSED MOVEMENTS SHOWN THIS BOOK ARE ENOUGH, OR IF YOU NEED THE "ISOSTRETCH" BOOK.

WHAT IS MISSING FROM MOST WEIGHT LOSS PLANS?

WE'VE BEEN TOLD <u>WHAT</u> TO DO, <u>BUT NOT HOW</u> TO!

WEIGHT LOSS PLANS DON'T SHOW HOW TO USE COMMON SENSE TO MAKE THEM <u>PAINLESS AND FUN</u>.

THEY DON'T HAVE THE EASY "ISOSTRETCH" PROGRAM TO HELP THEM.

<u>ONLY YOU CAN CHANGE YOUR LIFESTYLE</u>. <u>USE COMMON SENSE</u>!

NO ONE CAN DO IT FOR YOU. HOWEVER, YOU CAN BECOME A <u>SELF STARTER</u>; THE SUCCESS SECRET TO ACCOMPLISHING ANYTHING!

ONCE YOU BECOME A SELF STARTER, THE REST IS DOWNHILL!

THE EXERCISES BELOW, ALSO SHOWN WITH PICTURES IN MY BOOK, "ISOSTRETCH," ARE GENERAL GUIDES ONLY. DO ONLY THE ONES OR PARTS OF ONE THAT YOU CAN DO COMFORTABLY.

EVERYONE'S BODY IS DIFFERENT. IT TOOK A WHILE BEFORE I WAS ABLE TO COMPLETE A SET. THE MORE I DID, THE MORE I COULD DO.

YOU CAN'T DO THEM WRONG! MUSCLES LOVE CONFUSION! ISOSTRETCH IS A FEEL GOOD PROGRAM. SOME DAYS YOU JUST DON'T FEEL GOOD! DO LESS, BUT DO SOMETHING! USE COMMON SENSE!

DO ONLY WHAT IS COMFORTABLE TODAY AND YOU WILL FEEL GOOD ABOUT DOING IT TOMORROW.

WEIGHT LOSS, BODY SCULPTING AND A BETTER FITNESS LIFESTYLE ARE A BONUS.

YOU WILL FIND THAT YOU ARE LOOKING FORWARD TO YOUR ISOSTRETCHES.

YOU WILL NOT DREAD THE PAINFUL BORING EXERCISES YOU HAVE BEEN SUBJECTED TO FOR YEARS.

ISOSTRETCH SHOWS ALMOST EVERYONE, <u>EVEN DISABLED LIKE MYSELF, HOW TO GET STARTED.</u>

<u>STAY ON TRACK,</u> AND TO ENJOY A FUN AND EASY <u>EXERCISE FOR A LIFETIME OF FITNESS.</u> NO SURGERY! NO PILLS!   NO SWEAT!

YOU CAN GET MY FULL COLOR BOOK, "ISOSTRETCH," SHOWING PICTURES OF EXACTLY HOW THE EXERCISES ARE DONE.

THERE ARE SPECIFIC SECRETS ABOUT GOALS, EATING TIPS, POSITIVE THINKING, TIME USE, WILL POWER, MUSCLE MEMORY OF THE MIND. ETC.

<u>THE FOLLOWING MOVEMENTS</u> GIVE YOU A GENERAL VIEW OF THE EXERCISES IN THE "ISOSTRETCH" BOOK.

<u>SEE IF YOU CAN DO THEM</u> OR IF YOU NEED TO ORDER THE "ISOSTRETCH" BOOK.

THE "ISOSTRETCH" BOOK SHOWS <u>MORE DETAILED</u> MOVEMENTS.

A DVD VIDEO IS ALSO AVAILABLE TO "SEE" THE   MOVEMENTS.

 THE PRICES FOR THE "ISOSTRETCH" BOOK AND VIDEO ARE $20

EACH OR BOTH FOR $35.

JIM MORROW

256-235-3889   BASICCOMMONSENSE@BELLSOUTH.NET

ISOSTRETCH INSTRUCTIONS.

<u>SLOW</u> AND <u>EASY</u> IS THE KEY. <u>DO ONLY</u> AS MANY AS <u>COMFORTABLE, RELAX.</u> <u>YOU DON'T</u> HAVE TO <u>DO THEM ALL AT ONE TIME.</u>

YOU <u>DON'T EVEN</u> HAVE TO <u>WORRY</u> ABOUT <u>DOING THEM RIGHT</u> OR THE CORRECT NUMBER. THE BODY <u>LOVES CONFUSION!</u>

<u>I USED A BELT AROUND MY LOWER BACK FOR SUPPORT DOING MOVEMENTS AT FIRST. FEEL FREE TO DO THE SAME.</u>

WARM UP. ROLL AROUND ON THE BED. STRETCH YOUR ARMS AND LEGS, BEND OVER ON THE SIDE OF THE BED A FEW TIMES.

FROM NOW ON, WHEN I SAY NUMBER OF REPS, IT ALSO MEANS: <u>TIGHTEN YOUR CORE</u> DURING REPS.

CORE MEANS YOUR BELLY AREA, UPPER AND

LOWER.

DO THE REPS WITH YOUR LEFT THUMB UNDER YOUR RIGHT IF YOU ARE ON YOUR LEFT SIDE.

GRIP TIGHT, PUSH OUTWARD WITH THE HAND WITH THE THUMB OVER. PULL IN WITH THE HAND THAT HAS THE THUMB UNDER ON EVERY EXERCISE. ALTERNATE, IF HANDS ARE STRAIGHT AHEAD.

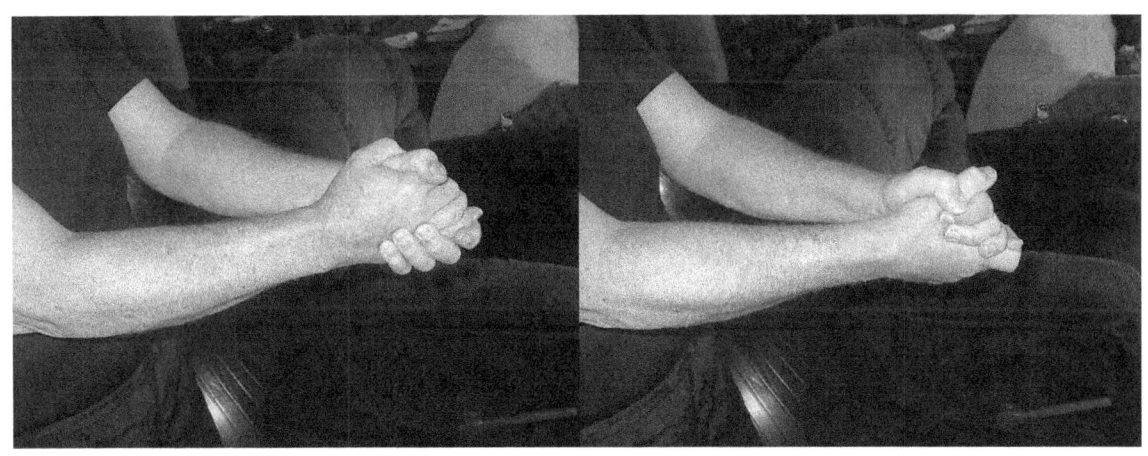

YOUR RIGHT THUMB UNDER YOUR LEFT IF YOU ARE ON YOUR RIGHT SIDE.

A KEY COMPONENT OF ISOSTRETCH EXERCISES IS <u>TIGHTENING YOUR CORE</u> AND RELEASING; <u>THEN RELAXING.</u>

DAILY EXERCISES. A FULL COLOR VIDEO AND MY "ISOSTRETCH BOOK WITH EXACT PICTURES OF THE MOVEMENTS ARE AVAILABLE IF YOU CANNOT UNDERSTAND THESE INSTRUCTIONS.

THE FOLLOWING MAY BE SHOWN ON A BED OR CHAIR TO SAVE PICTURES; BUT, YOU CAN DO THE SAME EXERCISES ON A BED OR CHAIR.

EVEN IF THE PICTURES SHOW ME SITTING; YOU CAN DO THEM ON YOUR BACK OR SIDES MOST OF THE TIME.

I USE PILLOWS UNDER MY RUMP SOMETIMES BECAUSE IT IS EASY ON MY BACK.

1. THIS IS A NEW EXERCISE I USE SINCE MY ISOSTRETCH BOOK! CLASP HANDS, BEND OVER KNEE PLACED ON BED AS FAR AS COMFORTABLE WITH OTHER FOOT ON FLOOR. TIGHTEN CORE, 10 REPS. DO AS FEW AS NEEDED TO START! IF IT HURTS, DO ONE A DAY TILL IT IS EASIER. MY BEST CORE AND BACK EXERCISE!

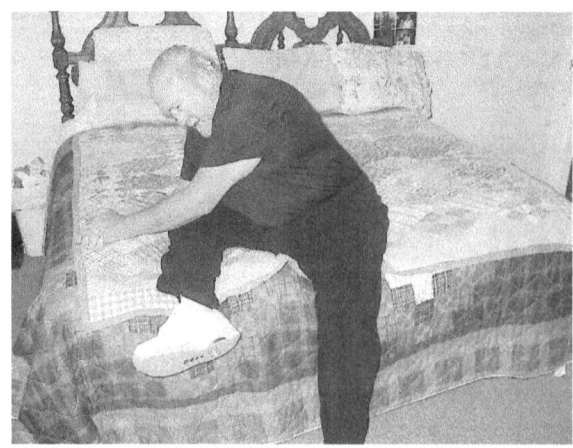

DO IT THE SAME WAY ON THE OTHER SIDE. I CAN NOW BEND

FROM SITTING UP STRAIGHT, TO ALL THE WAY DOWN, WITH MY FACE TOUCHING BED. I COULD NOT GO HALFWAY WHEN I STARTED.

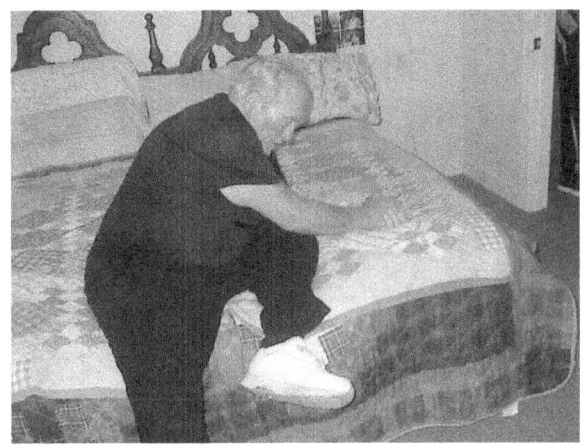

2. IN CHAIR, PUT LEFT HAND ACROSS RIGHT BICEP, PULL WHILE TIGHTENING CORE. REPEAT THE OTHER ARM. 10 REPS.

3. ON BACK,CLASP HANDS ARMS ABOVEHEAD, TIGHTEN BORE FOR TEN SECONDS, RELAX. 10 REPS

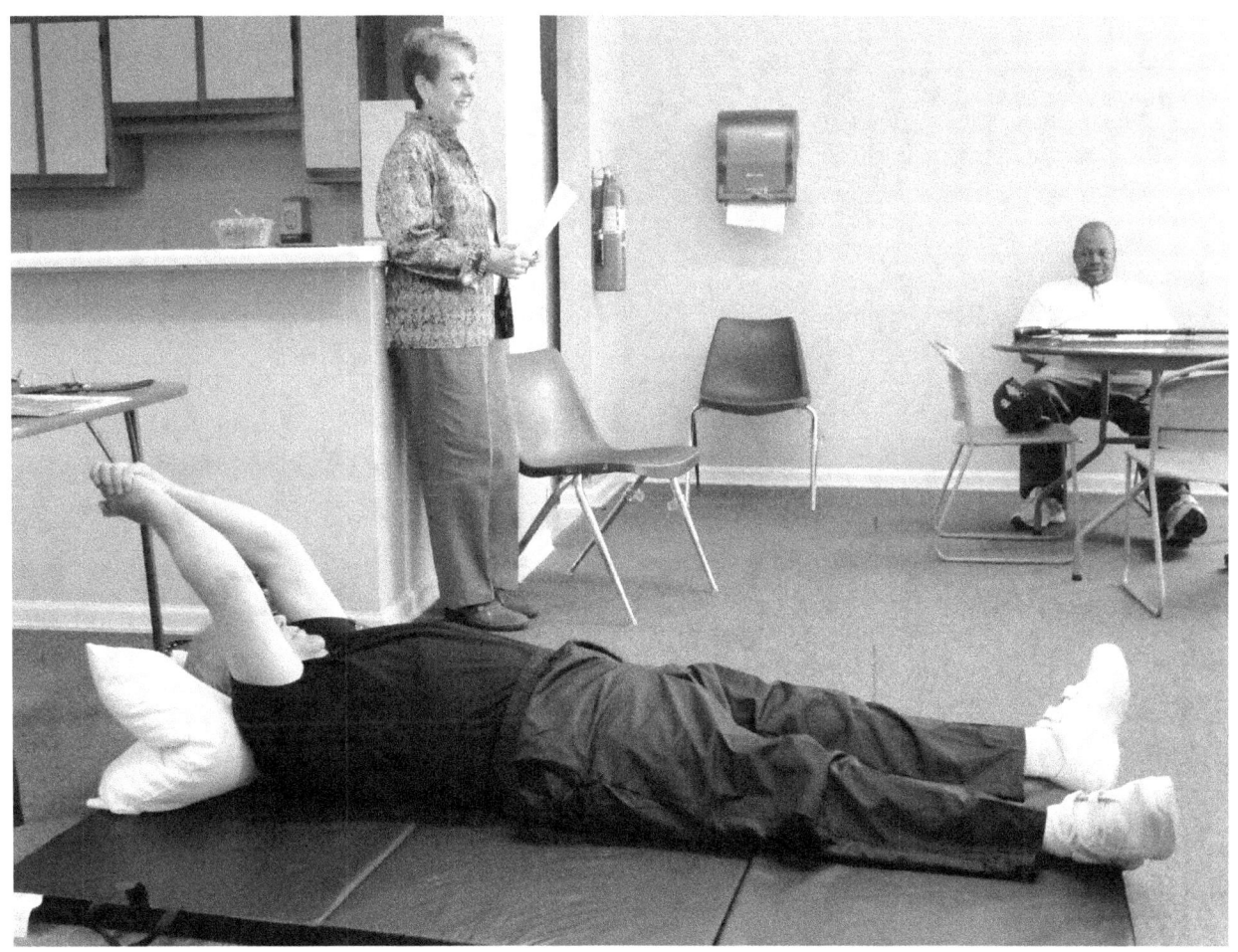

ON YOUR LEFT SIDE, CLASP HANDS, LEFT THUMB UNDER RIGHT, RAISE YOUR ARMS ABOVE YOUR HEAD AT A 45 DEGREE ANGLE. TIGHTEN CORE AND RELEASE. 10 REPS.

RECLASP, DO THE SAME ON THE OTHER SIDE. RIGHT SIDE,

MOVE ARMS ABOVE HEAD AT A 45 DEGREE ANGLE. CLASP HANDS, 10 REPS. REPEAT OTHER SIDE.

4. ON BACK, ELBOWS IN, HANDS UP, PRESS DOWN. 10 REPS. MASSAGE STOMACH, BELLY AND LOWER AREA 2 MINUTES.

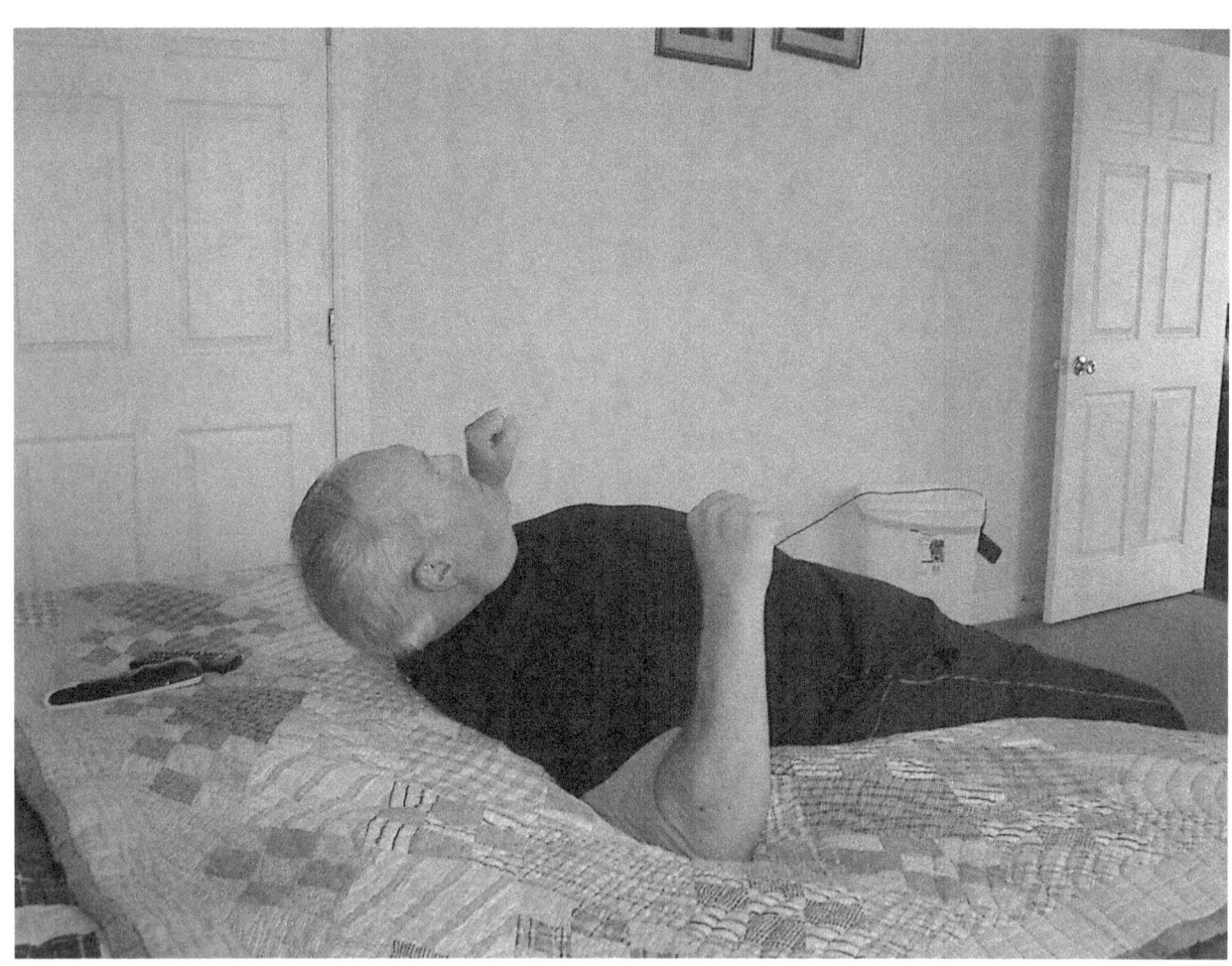

5. ON BACK, PUT RIGHT HAND OVER LEFT BICEP, PULL, DO 10 REPS.

THE PICTURE SHOWS SITTING, TO SHOW GRIPS, BUT YOU CAN ALSO LAY ON YOUR BACK.

6. ROLL ON YOUR RIGHT SIDE, CLASP HANDS WITH RIGHT THUMB UNDER LEFT, DRAW HANDS AND ARMS TO CHEST. TIGHTEN CORE, TEN REPS. CHANGE HANDGRIPS, DO THE SAME ON YOUR LEFT SIDE.

THIS PICTURE SHOWS SITTING TO SHOW GRIPS, BUT YOU CAN ALSO LAY ON YOUR BACK.

7. ON BACK, PUNCH LIKE A BOXER. 20 REPS.

THIS PICTURE SHOWS SITTING TO SHOW GRIPS, BUT YOU CAN ALSO LAY ON YOUR BACK.

8. ON BACK, THROW BASEBALL. 20 REPS. TIGHTEN CORE.

THIS PICTURE SHOWS SITTING TO SHOW GRIPS, BUT YOU CAN ALSO LAY ON YOUR BACK. YOU CAN DO THIS AND THE PREVIOUS MOVEMENTS IN A CHAIR IF PREFERRED.

9 . SITTING, DO CURLS, 10 REPS EACH ARM. TIGHTEN CORE.

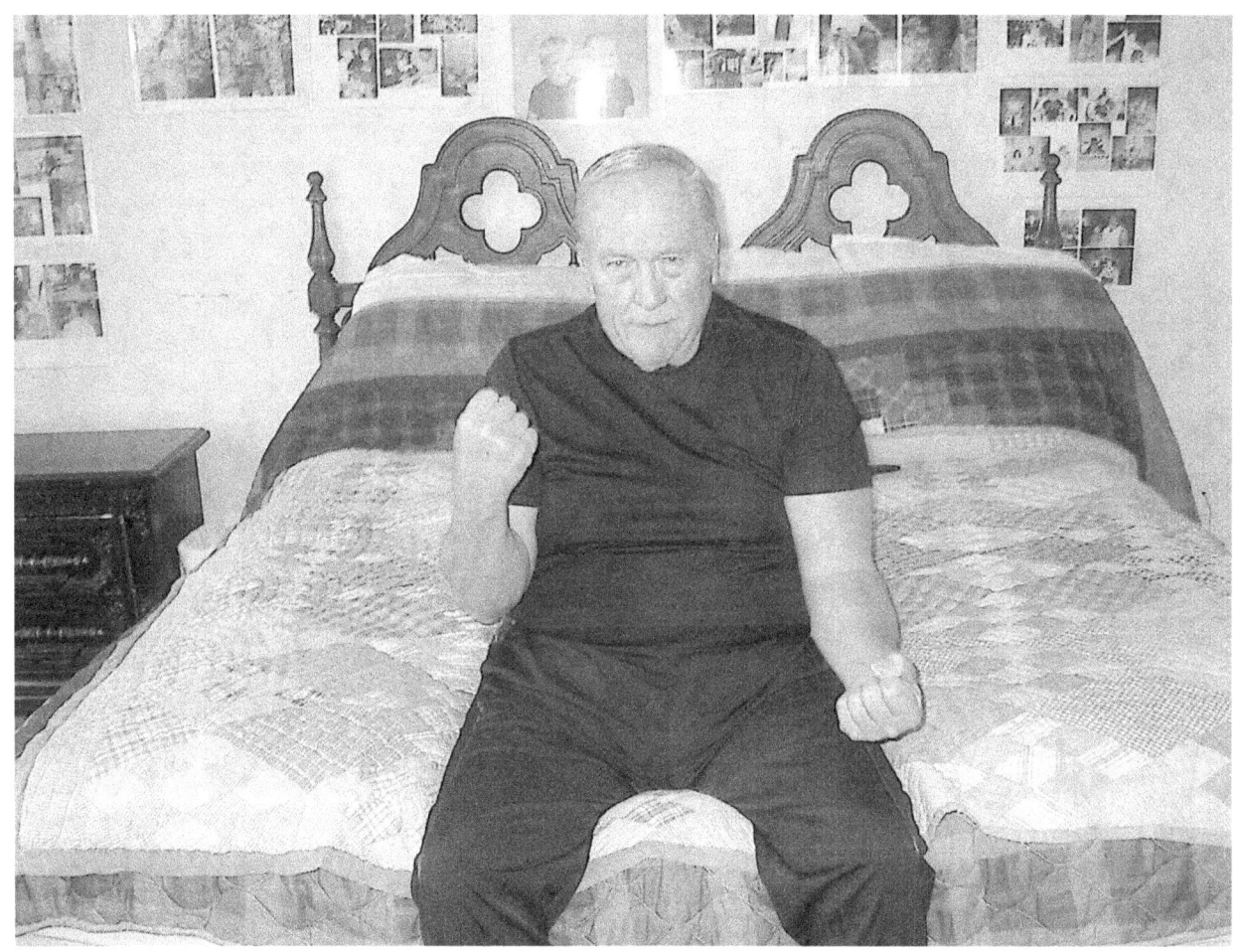

PLEASE SEE PILLOWS SHOWN IN FIGURE 14 FOR THE FOLLOWING EXERCISES.

10. WITH 3 PILLOWS UNDER YOUR BUTT WHILE ON YOUR BACK, ARMS OVERHEAD TIGHTEN RUMP AND CORE 20 REPS.

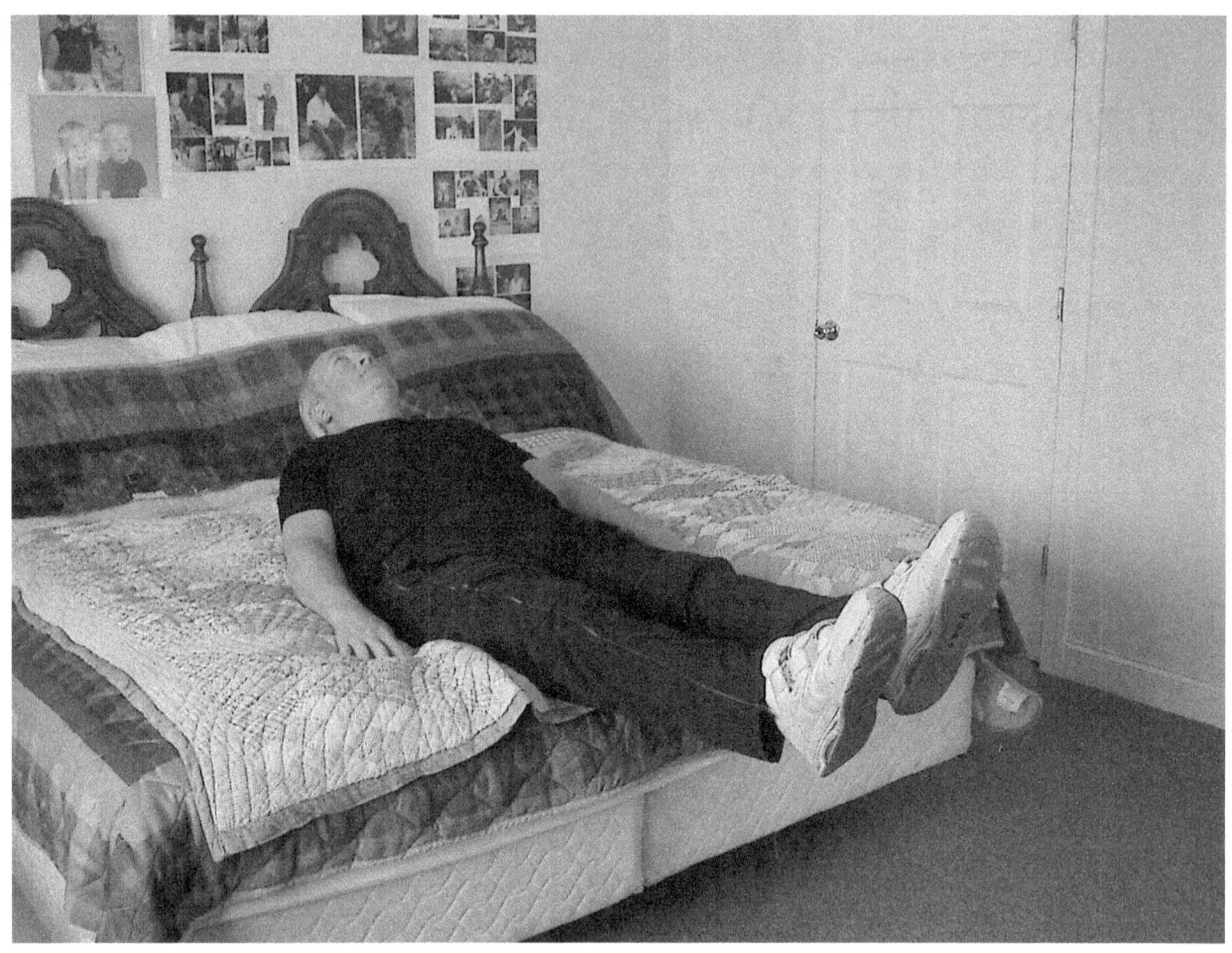

THIS PICTURE DOES NOT SHOW PILLOWS, BUT THEY ARE ESSENTIAL TO THE MOVEMENT.

11. STILL ON PILLOWS, GRAB KNEES PULL TO CHEST 10 REPS. THIS IS GREAT FOR ABS WITH OUT THE STRAIN OF SIT-UPS AND BACK PAIN. TIGHTEN CORE.

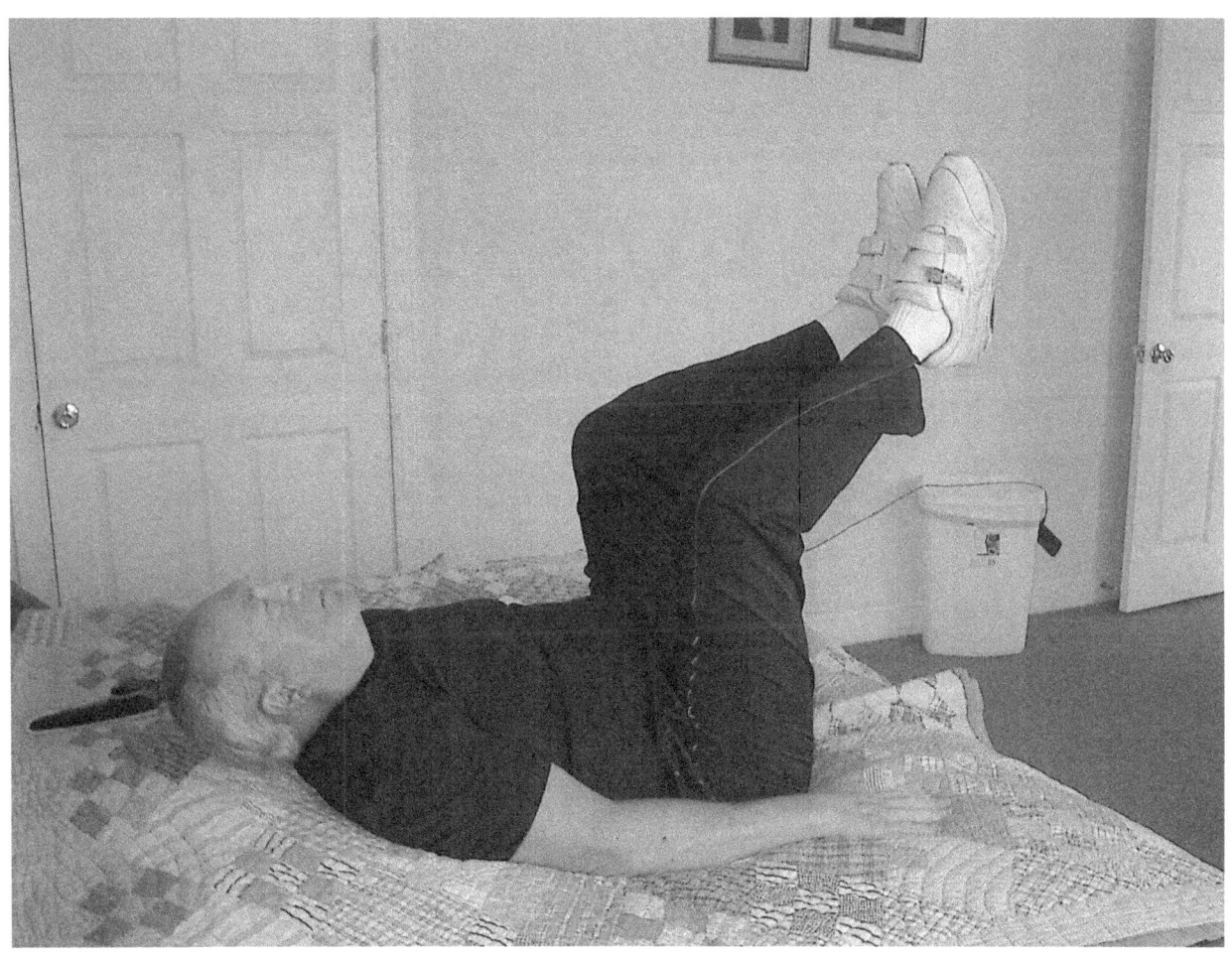

USE PILLOWS

12. ROCK SIDE TO SIDE 10 TIMES. TIGHTEN CORE.

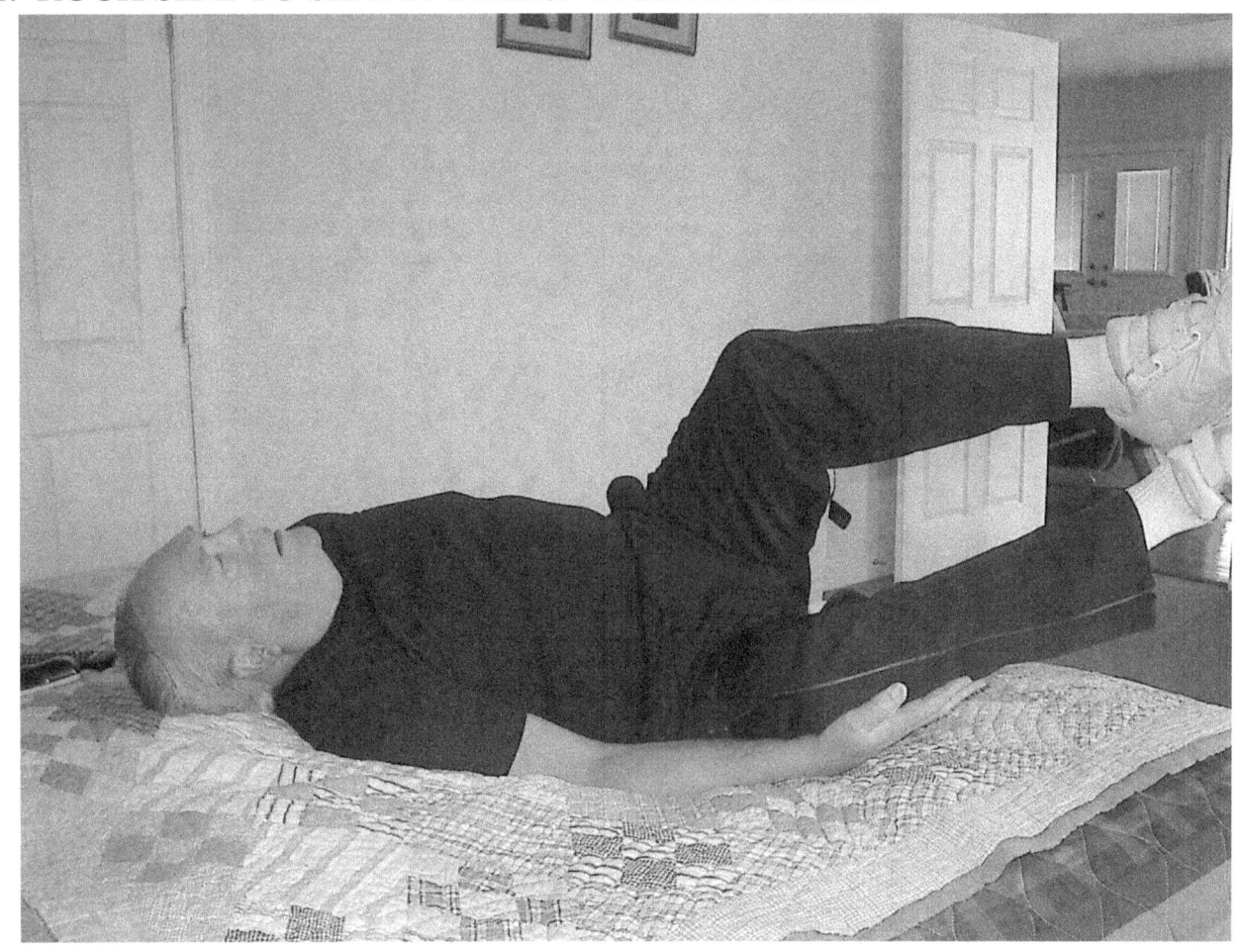

ROCK SIDE TO SIDE STRETCH LEGS AT 45 DEGREES. 10 REPS.

USE PILLOWS

13. KICK FOOTBALL 10 REPS EACH LEG TIGHTEN CORE.

USE PILLOWS

THIS IS THE ONLY REAL AEROBIC EXERCISE I USE. ADJUST REPS FOR HOW MUCH YOU NEED, AND HOW MUCH YOU CAN DO.

14. RIDE BICYCLE UPSIDE DOWN 50 REPS. USE PILLOWS

THESE <u>LAST TWO EXERCISES</u> AND <u>THE NEW EXERCISE</u> PICTURED FIRST HAVE BEEN A <u>LIFE-SAVER</u> FOR ME. I COULD <u>NOT WALK</u> OR EVEN RIDE A BIKE <u>COMFORTABLY</u> BECAUSE OF MY BACK AND WEIGHT. <u>I COULD NOT DO SIT-UPS; ANYTHING STRENUOUS</u>!

I STARTED THEM <u>SLOWLY</u> AND FOUND THAT I COULD KICK AND RIDE UPSIDE DOWN FOR A <u>FEW REPS</u>. DO ONLY WHAT YOU CAN <u>WITHOUT STRAIN</u> AT THE START, THEN BUILD TO WHATEVER IS <u>STILL COMFORTABLE</u>, BUT DO IT <u>DAILY</u>!

MY <u>BACK BUILT UP WITHOUT PAIN; I WALK AGAIN</u>, AND I LOST ONE AND A HALF FEET IN THE <u>WAIST</u>, TIGHTENING MY CORE.

15. FEET ON FLOOR, TOUCH FLOOR, OR AS FAR AS YOU CAN, AS MANY AS YOU CAN, COMFORTABILITY.   YOU PROBABLY WILL NOT BE ABLE TO TIGHTEN CORE IF YOU ARE REAL BIG LIKE I WAS.   WAIT UNTIL YOU LOSE WEIGHT AND YOU CAN TIGHTEN IT COMFORTABLY.

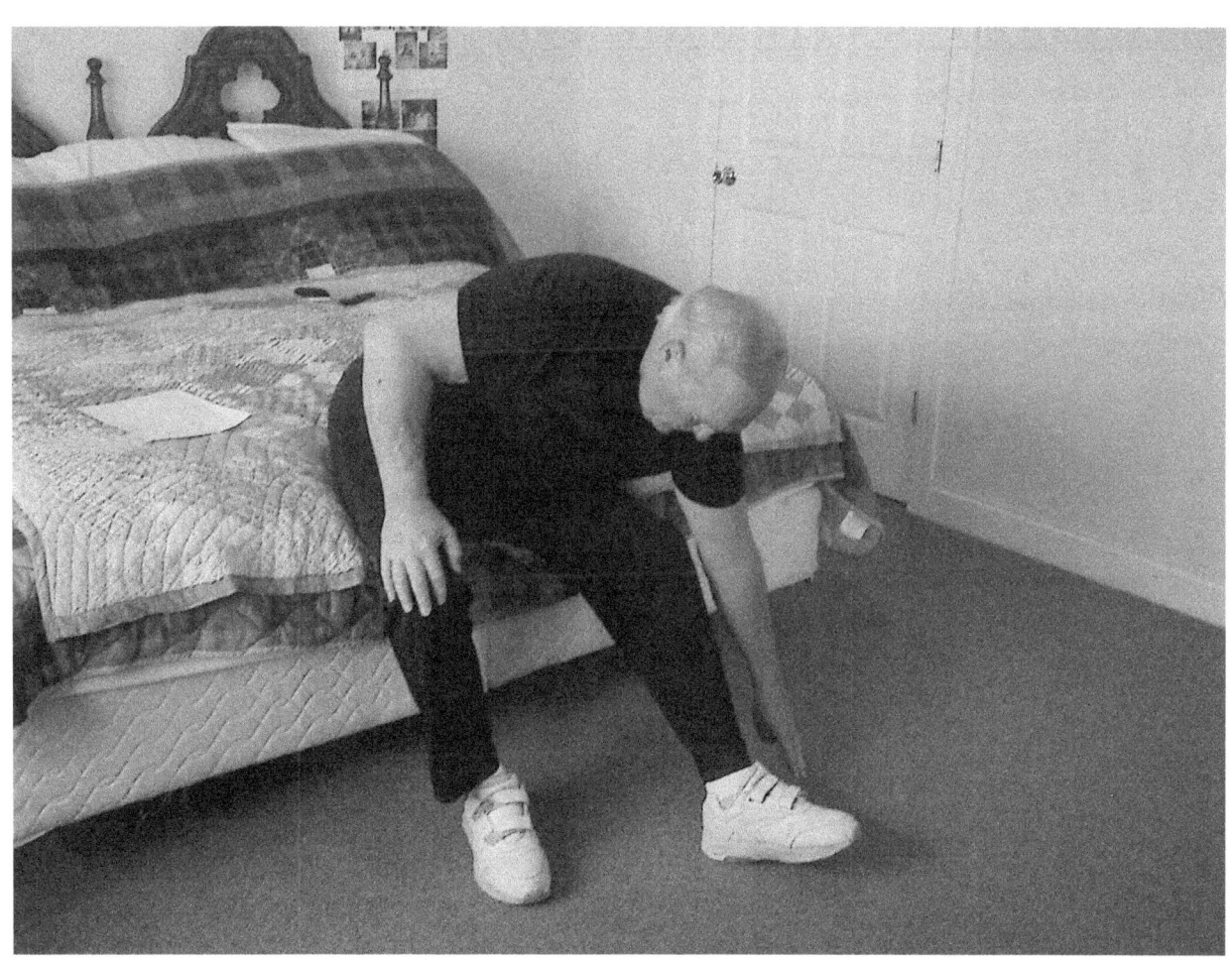

FEET ON FLOOR, EDGE OF THE BED, BEND OVER RIGHT AND LEFT KNEE 5 TIMES.

SITTING, ON EDGE OF BED, RAISE ALTERNATE KNEES WALKING IN PLACE, 10 REPS.

IT IS IMPORTANT THAT WHEN YOU USE ISOSTRETCH, THAT YOU ARE COMFORTABLE, <u>DO NOT STRAIN AND ENJOY YOUR EXERCISE</u>.

YOU WILL EVENTUALLY DROP ANY PROGRAM THAT YOU DREAD DOING EVERY DAY.

IF YOU WOULD RATHER DO THE EXERCISES IN A CHAIR THAN ON A BED, YOU CAN. ANYWHERE, ANY TIME OF THE DAY; <u>YOU DON'T HAVE TO DO THEM ALL AT ONE TIME!</u>

16. HANDS OVER HEAD, TIGHTEN BUTTOCKS 10 REPS, BREATHE.

IN CHAIR, RAISE ARMS ABOVE HEAD, TIGHTEN CORE FOR 10
SECONDS, RELAX. 10 REPS IN CHAIR, ON YOUR LEFT SIDE,
CLASP HANDS, LEFT THUMB UNDER RIGHT, RAISE YOUR ARMS
ABOVE YOUR HEAD AT A 45 DEGREE ANGLE. TIGHTEN CORE
AND RELEASE. 10 REPS.

RECLASP, DO THE SAME ON THE OTHER SIDE. RIGHT SIDE,
MOVE ARMS ABOVE HEAD AT A 45 DEGREE ANGLE. CLASP

HANDS, 10 REPS. REPEAT OTHER SIDE.

17. RIGHT SIDE- CLASP HANDS NEAR CHEST-ISOSTRETCH CHANGE SIDES-10 REPS.

18.   IN CHAIR, ON YOUR LEFT SIDE, CLASP HANDS, LEFT THUMB UNDER RIGHT, RAISE YOUR ARMS ABOVE YOUR HEAD AT A 45 DEGREE ANGLE. TIGHTEN CORE AND RELEASE. 10 REPS.

RECLASP, DO THE SAME ON THE OTHER SIDE. RIGHT SIDE, MOVE ARMS ABOVE HEAD AT A 45 DEGREE ANGLE.   CLASP HANDS, 10 REPS. REPEAT OTHER SIDE.

READ MY BOOK "ISOSTRETCH" TODAY AND FIND

OUT WHY I THINK IT SAVED MY LIFE! <u>SEE THE COVER BELOW SHOWING THE BELT I USED TO USE!</u>

I LOST A FOOT AND A HALF IN THE WAIST!

A DVD VIDEO IS ALSO AVAILABLE TO "SEE" THE MOVEMENTS.

THE PRICES FOR THE BOOK AND VIDEO ARE $20 EACH OR BOTH FOR $35.

LOSING WEIGHT AND LIFETIME FITNESS PLANS ARE TOPICS THAT I WILL PERSONALLY CONSULT WITH YOU, YOUR GROUP OR EMPLOYEES, ON SITE, OR BY TELEPHONE. I WILL EVEN BRING

THE BELT!

FIFTY YEARS OF EXPERIENCE IS AVAILABLE AT VERY REASONABLE RATES. AS OF THIS DATE, FEB. 10, CONSULTATION RATES ARE $150 PER HOUR PLUS EXPENSES.

NO CONSULTATION IS TOO SMALL OR TOO LARGE. I HAVE OWNED AND MANAGED SEVERAL ONE MAN BUSINESSES, AND UP TO TWELVE MILLION DOLLAR DEVELOPMENTS.

I HAD TO START MY BUSINESSES ALONE. I NOW REALIZE, THE VALUE OF OTHER PEOPLE'S POINTS OF VIEW; AND EVEN AS A 73-YEAR-OLD, I STILL USE THEM.

I FINALLY USED MY COMMON SENSE TO TACKLE WEIGHT LOSS. I HAD BEEN OBESE FOR 45 YEARS. MY COMMON SENSE WEIGHT LOSS AND FITNESS DISCOVERY PROBABLY SAVED MY LIFE.

I DEVELOPED THE ISOSTRETCH SYSTEM FOR MYSELF AND TO SHOW OTHERS THAT WE CAN OVERCOME DISASTERS AND DISABILITIES AND STILL REACH OUR GOALS.

I PERSONALLY GIVE THE CREDIT FOR MY SUCCESS TO MY BROTHER BOB AND TO A MOTIVATIONAL SPEAKER, ZIG ZIGLAR. I LEARNED THINGS THAT I STILL USE DAILY.

SOMETIMES A GOOD MOTIVATIONAL CONSULTATION IS NEEDED TO GET US STARTED. IT IS ALSO ASSURES OURSELVES THAT WE ARE AS GOOD AS ANYONE AND CAN DO ANYTHING THAT OUR MINDS CAN IMAGINE.

FOR INDIVIDUAL OR GROUP CONSULTATIONS,
CONTACT JIM@COMMONSENSECOMMENTARY.COM

JIM MORROW

BASICCOMMONSENSE@BELLSOUTH.NET

THESE IMMEDIATE REFERENCE BOOKLETS ARE ALSO AVAILABLE:

1. "WRITE IT DOWN"

2. "DON'T ASSUME"

3. "HOW TO SELL ANYTHING IN 10 SECONDS",

4. "HOW TO SELL ANYTHING IN THREE LITTLE WORDS",

5. "SALES MANUAL FOR ANY BUSINESS", "GENERAL ADVERTISING",

6. "HOW TO SELL A BUSINESS',

7. "HOW TO BUY A BUSINESS",

8. "LEARN HOW TO BECOME A REAL ESTATE SALES PERSON IN 30

MINUTES AND KEEP IT FOREVER",

9. "HOW THREE SECRET WORDS CAN SAVE OR MAKE YOU MILLIONS IN REAL ESTATE, (THEY ARE NOT LOCATION, LOCATION, LOCATION).

10. "THE ONE SECRET TO BEGINNING A NEW BUSINESS QUICKLY AND SUCCESSFULLY THAT 99% OF THE PEOPLE DON'T KNOW ABOUT".

TO ORDER THESE BOOKLETS (FIVE DOLLARS), CLICK JIM@COMMONSENSECOMMENTARY.COM.

BEFORE 375 LBS   AFTER 225 LBS